GERMAN BAROQUE ART

G. Schütz.

THE BELVEDERE GARDEN, VIENNA.

GERMAN BAROQUE ART

BY

SACHEVERELL SITWELL

AUTHOR OF "SOUTHERN BAROQUE ART"

LONDON
DUCKWORTH
3 HENRIETTA STREET
1927

Printed in Great Britain
by The Riverside Press Limited
Edinburgh

TO
W. T. W.

LIST OF ILLUSTRATIONS

List of Illustrations

The medallion on the title page is from a silver coin of the Emperor Leopold I.

8

PREFACE

This book is in no sense meant as a companion volume to a previous publication of mine—*Southern Baroque Art*. Here I have been moved by but one consideration—that there is no book in our language dealing with the Baroque Architecture of Central Europe. Therefore, this book has taken the form of a catalogue of places and objects; but, at the same time, while moving on a prescribed tour round the country I have tried to group together works by the same man so that architects like Fischer von Erlach or J. B. Neumann appear as definite figures.

The first half of the illustrations is reproduced from old books, and the second half has been selected from the innumerable recent German books on the subject. I have put a number of old and modern books worth studying in the Bibliography at the end so as to try to give scope to anyone who wishes to pursue a deeper study of the period. It has been my aim to make the works of the great Germans, Fischer von Erlach, Lukas von Hildebrandt, Kilian Ignaz Dientzenhofer, J. B. Neumann, J. M. Fischer, and the brothers Egid Quirin and Cosmas Damian Asam, as familiar as those of Bernini. Beyond that ambition these pages have but little pretence to any literary importance.

The architecture and the culture of which this book treats will come as a revelation of beauty to many people who, however much the names of Bach, of Handel, of Haydn, of Mozart, may mean to them, had never suspected, or would not believe, that those geniuses had been supported by an equivalent architecture and beauty of life. That such was the case is sufficiently proved by the illustrations of this book; while should I have managed to interpolate some information upon their creators my incentive to this difficult labour will have been rewarded.

It is my ambition to prepare two similar volumes on the Baroque Architecture of the old Kingdom of Naples, and of Spain, Portugal, and the ancient colonies of those countries in Central and South America. The available material has been enormously increased of late; there is a whole corpus of architectural photographs of Mexico from which to choose, while there are old cities in Brazil, in the states of Minas Geraes and São Paolo, which are now beginning to be studied; cities like Ouro Preto with its seven churches and many palaces, like Marianna, or like Cachoeira do Campo, are as full of interest as a second Mexico, and this remote part of the world produced its great craftsmen like Aleijadinho, a cripple who had no hands and working with tools strapped to his wrists carved pulpits, confessionals, altar-screens, and statues, all over the state of Minas Geraes.

It is only possible for me in this last paragraph of preface to hope that the intense interest and pleasure that have spurred me on may be communicated in some degree to the readers of this book, and that their support of this enterprise will be a guarantee for the appearance of the two promised volumes. It is the fault, neither of the author, nor of his present publishers, that this book has been so long delayed in the press. It should have appeared three years ago, and now makes a late but revised appearance armed with this excuse and these various ambitions.

21st July 1927.

I

The Historical Scene

ANEW chalky white castle with high-gabled red roofs rises straight in front up a little slope. The air is crisp and clean so that you can almost smell the newness of paint and woodwork. It is a huge affair rambling all over the place, flying in and out round every contrived corner that ingenuity can devise. But if you will only climb the slope a little higher up, or, in default of that, scale one of these briary trees near by, you are rewarded with the whole secret of this immediate romanticism, for a pointed and angular poetry clings to every detail of the scene. Now it stands revealed—in a flat, blue flash—and all those castle walls and towers come climbing out of the waters of a lake, for the whole is built on a little reedy islet.

Everything about it seems new, the beams and paint are as fresh as spring, and even the water and the trees have a pretence of youth. A river just in front runs down to feed the lake, and this turbulent melted rush presents the most extraordinary spectacle. It is filled with hundreds of many-antlered deer, who are struggling desperately from bank to bank under a shower of arrows, and with the smoky banging of innumerable guns making them plunge more wildly still in their panic. Their enemies are a number of bearded huntsmen dressed in different gradations of green, as though matched against the grass, or the graded liveries of the trees as they descend from spring freshness into the fat, blackish girth of summer. A particular group, more

11

richly dressed, would seem to be in supervision of this massacre. Hounds are baying, and the blowing of hunting-horns, more loud even than the belling of the deer, leaves but a moment to compare the bearded fatness of one man with that other, more familiar, bearded dreaminess, heavy eyes and loaded jutting chin. In the meantime a feast of giant proportions is being prepared in the chapel-like kitchens of the castle, to be succeeded, of course, by a monotonous drunkenness.

These are the Northern and crepuscular distances to which Roman Emperors have travelled. That pointed and pre-eminent chin is the hieratic mark that distinguishes the Hapsburg family, and this is its most famous member, Charles V. He is hunting with the Elector Maurice of Saxony at the Moritzburg, near Dresden—a castle which had been built only three years before, in 1541. This river, fed from Saxon snows, flows away into the Baltic, and the plains of Poland are only a little way removed, while we may be certain that a great many of these green-clad huntsmen have the flat-backed Slavonic heads that seem meant to be left about on a battle-field.

This is a long way from the marshes of Ravenna, to which Honorius fled, or from Constantinople, the other half of the Roman inheritance, that drew a great part of its wealth from the Asiatic Pontine shores and collected a turbaned and hawk-nosed metropolitan population as divergent as are the races that fill New York, while the Emperors of Byzantium lived in a world of Persian luxury and of Jewish or Armenian attachment to the precious metals. This dynasty, whose fortunes we are following, have fled a long way from the former double-capitals of the world into what used to be barbarian fastnesses, but have now become the centres of trade. Cities on that bleak and marshy fringe opposite Britain have now twisted and gilded their fretwork pinnacles into a filagree that we must accept as an equivalent symbol to the massed effects of Byzantium for an indication of wealth and luxury. Bruges and Ghent, having fallen to Charles in inheritance, are the riches of this modern Roman world, that is so soon to be given a final and hopeless expansion over the whole of the globe with the discovery of America and the Indies. Then, by marriage, the net will be spread over France, Portugal, Hungary, England; and just when omnipotence seems assured, various marriages will prove fruitless, different vassals will revolt, and the whole of this vast inheritance will be once more divided when it seemed as if the Republic of Venice and the Sultan of Turkey were the only possible exceptions to its rule.

All this is to come in a few years : Charles, whom we see here in Northern Germany, will retire to Spain, keeping only Milan, Naples, and the Netherlands for his children's inheritance, together with America, while his brother Maximilian succeeds to all the Germanic possessions of the family. Just at this moment we see him, as I have described, in Saxony, and our authority is the painter Lucas Cranach the Younger ; while the two views of this hunting party with the Moritzburg in the background are to be seen in the room of the German Masters in the Prado at Madrid.

They are bad pictures ; but they serve our purpose by showing us just what we require, the mediæval capriciousness of Germany curving out and bursting into a strange and redundant protuberance, which was their interpretation of the classic, and which corresponds, where such places as the Moritzburg are concerned, to the Château of Chambord, or to some of the great Elizabethan houses of England. A building of this nature—take, for instance, the castle at Heidelberg—is the key to the whole of an age, and we fasten, therefore, upon such transitional landmarks as these in our consideration of the birth of that particular movement we are studying.

We are concerned, here, only with the German portions of the great Hapsburg inheritance, and so I have chosen as the starting-point these two pictures in the Prado, for they show us the Emperor in his most Teutonic surroundings, not very long before he retired from this part of the world to Spain. The great men of the German Renaissance were dead, and art and painting had collapsed, in the case of the latter, permanently, for the most Germanophile of critics can hardly put forward Chodowiecki or Tischbein as great or important masters. Both Dürer and Holbein were gone, and a period of strange and distorted taste was in progress. There is a frenzied angularity about the details of ornament : the Augsburg goldsmiths were in the midst of their microscopic achievement ; there was a great deal of indifferent stained glass being made ; there were elaborate woodcuts in the Dürer tradition still engraved and sold ; and perhaps German art was most successful when it concerned itself with heraldry. Armour grew more and more elaborate in its shape and finish, while such things as cannon were cast in the form of dragons till war became ornamentally terrifying as it was practised by the Chinese. Large and florid women were admired, while the female sex required their lovers to have full beards like those portly and robust forms we see on Flemish tapestry. Some of the German Ducal families, to judge by portraits, had by now attained through dynastic marriages to a truly portentous pitch of ugliness, and where the Hapsburg chin was the model of nobility we may conceive some of the lesser families breeding expressly for large noses, low foreheads, or some other family peculiarity over which heredity could be esteemed.

14

The German work corresponding in date to the reign of our Queen Elizabeth is of portentous and unsurpassed elaboration. It is founded upon the Flemish style of the time, but there was much money to be spent and patrons were not satisfied except with microscopic finish. The church and the castle at Bückeburg, the capital of the principality of Schaumburg-Lippe, may be taken as the most profitable example of what these means achieved in the direction of prodigal labour. Both church and palace show the influence of the architect Wendel Dietterlin. This strange person was born at Strassburg in 1550 and died at Stuttgart in 1599. He was invited to Stuttgart by Duke Ludwig of Würtemberg to build a Lusthaus. This was completed in 1593, and while at Stuttgart Dietterlin published his book on architecture, which had an immense influence on the age and gave birth to a whole race of crowded and monstrous buildings. Such redundant ornament never issued from any brain save that of Dietterlin ; in fact, his work is a mass of "conceits" in the strictly poetical sense of the word, and the designs in his book and the buildings that his influence inspired should be considered with the poetry of the period. The German authors of that school are necessarily unknown to me, but I feel tolerably certain of the truth of this parallel.

The prosperity which had been the source of such prolix activities now reached its height, and the whole system came crashing down in a series of religious broils, ending in the Thirty Years' War. This mad contest left the whole German world dead and exhausted, so that nothing more was to happen where art was concerned till towards the close of the next century. In fact, we may conceive the whole period of activity with which we are dealing to have started after the siege of Vienna by the Turks, at approximately the year 1685. We find ourselves,

15

therefore, in the reign of Leopold I. (1658-1705), and our period lasts till the death of Maria Theresa, in 1780—about a century.

Now Germany, so very unlike the results of that policy of centralisation affected by Louis XIV., has a vast number of semi-capital cities, and because of this there is a great variety of styles. Bavarian work is rather different from Prussian, or Austrian; but this latter country, as the residence of the Emperor, was the source and centre of the whole movement. Also, Vienna was not far from Italy, so that the Viennese were the first to benefit from the changes of Italian taste. It was far richer than any Italian town, and in fact the Emperor was the most important of European potentates, for Spain had by now sunk into poverty, and Louis XIV. was seen as an ambitious parvenu by the Cæsarean Court. They did really consider themselves as the heirs of the Cæsars, and the heads of the whole European system, with their position sanctified by nearly three centuries of hereditary right over and above their elective position.

The study of the age in which these pretensions existed discovers many important psychological facts about how absolute rule can be applied and to what limits it may be carried. We see the degree to which a human being can be invested with a hieratic importance quite irrelevant to his actual qualities, and whether such a process of falsification has really the faults that would seem necessary to its working. The procedure of this hero-worship is the cause of a great outlet of human activity in the arts, and these, perhaps, rather theatrical purposes are nowhere carried into a more detailed and profuse execution than in Germany. The Spaniards, who might have done this sort of thing with more elegance, had not the wealth at their disposal, and so a certain process may be seen in Germany carried to its extreme limits with a maximum of means and a minimum of talent. These things considered, it is quite extraordinary to note the excellence to which many architects of inferior powers were able to attain through working in a manner that was strict and yet free in its application. We find several men to whom we may attribute powers not inferior to our own Vanbrugh, and a profusion of good work that no other country has to offer at this period. In fact, the Baroque style is the most logical and native form of German expression, and this bastard and romanticised classicism was the method by which the later Holy Roman Empire emphasised a dying cause by disproportionate monuments. National feeling in Germany was nearly non-existent and dynastic interests had absolutely swamped every other consideration, so that the Cæsarean pretension of the Hapsburgs, which they based on a long descent, was of more importance to them, however unreal it might be, than the cultivation of German patriotism.

This kind of romantic ancestor-worship can never have been carried further—in its logical manifestations—than in Germany. Marriages were arranged without any other aspect whatever save pedigree and the number of quarterings inherited, and it is safe to conclude that life was duller and more restricted—save for its magnificent externals — than it is possible to imagine. People whose claim to your friendship is their number of quarterings make poor company.

This fevered claim to Imperial rule, however thin and dwindled in its chances, was supported with the utmost science of extravagance. Prelates became Princes, monasteries were built like palaces, and nobles and monks between them owned most of the wealth of the country. It must be conceded that they left more behind them than we have to show in England for that Golden Age of peace and prosperity, the nineteenth century. The quite limitless wealth of the vast Hapsburg dominions found expression in fine architecture and in the niceties of ceremony and dress. Against this refinement are to be set the most brutal bull-fights, and animal-contests of a more than Spanish cruelty—bears let loose in the circus to attack and eat young bullocks—cock-fights, and other evidences of the sporting instinct.

Vienna was more than the capital of Germany; there were not only the rich German vassals of the Empire living there, but also the magnates of Bohemia and Hungary, many Italians from Milan, and, later on in the century, a final addition to this diversified throng in the shape of those of the Polish nobles who had now to pay allegiance to Vienna after the partition of their wretched country. The retainers of all these wore their national costume; coaches lurched along the ill-paved streets with two servants in Hungarian Hussar-dress, two Trabants, or Heiducks, decked with Turkish scimitars on the step behind. There were Croats and Slovenes, Galicians, and nobles from Transylvania, in a kind of permanent rotation from the provinces to the capital. The Emperor's bodyguard, divided into different corps, brightened the streets with their dazzling uniforms. The German Guard wore red, with collar and facings of black velvet, the whole richly ornamented with gold lace; the Galician Guard was, at first, a cavalry corps dressed in the Polish costume; the Traban Guard wore red ornamented with gold lace, with white waistcoat and breeches; but all of these paled before the Hungarian Life Guard. This was quartered in the palace that Fischer von Erlach built for Prince Trautson; they wore a scarlet Hussar uniform enriched with silver lace, a tiger-skin pelisse, high yellow boots, and a high fur cap surmounted by a heron's plume, while their grey horses had green housings and silver bridles. Their colonel became, on appointment, a Baron of the Holy Roman Empire. This particular corps was founded under Maria Theresa, but her reign was a time of economy in comparison with the extravagance of her father and grandfather.

There are various books of engravings that show this city under just the aspects that we have been considering. We have been able to reproduce some illustrations by Salomon Kleiner and C. Schütz. The former of these shows Vienna in the reign of Charles VI., when this great era of building activity was still in progress. Kleiner has rendered the architecture with great success, and the streets are peopled with hundreds of figures, in the invention of which he has shown great humour and imagination. There are penitents loaded with chains and dragging great wooden crosses on their backs, processions of monks and nuns, dog-fights, harrowing groups of beggars, lackeys standing proudly in the doorways of their palaces, coaches with postilions, market-places full of stalls and vendors ; in fact the whole paraphernalia of a metropolis.

The other book is some half-century later in date, and the plates are hand-coloured with a rare minuteness. It is just the period of Mozart's operas ; the clipped hornbeams of Schönbrunn are by now high enough to afford a deep shade through the per-petual summer of this pleasant book, and the alleys are thronged with courtiers dressed in what are at once apparent as the newest of fashions. There are plates showing the Liechtenstein and Belvedere palaces, guard-mounting in the court of the Hofburg, and the aforementioned barrack of the Hungarian Noble Guard with some of those fiercely moustached paladins on sentry at the portal. The skies, I may add, are completely cloudless—as well they might be, for this undemocratic condition was to last for more than a century—till the death of old Franz Joseph. This book of Schütz is a good and picturesque documentation, tighter and more conscientious than the drawings of a Rowlandson, and with a sense of reverence towards the Great that was uncontaminated by a sense of humour. He must have spent many years over the preparation of this book, and we may feel doubtful as to the measure of success with which it met, since these elaborate works of a lifetime have generally a rapid collapse.

The best publisher of these books of views was the Augsburg firm of J. Wölff, and they employed engravers whose craft was in a direct descent from the great German technical experts of the Renaissance, for their plates are executed with a carefulness that is not typical of the age. They published another book from which I reproduce illustrations, the *Kurfürstlicher Baumeister*, by Paulus Decker the Elder, a wild feat of the imagination, comparable in scale to the pictures of Martin but of a scientific exactness based on long architectural practice and therefore of a just and reliable fantasy. It is a wild prodigy of fire and labour working together towards an intoxication of architecture, but it would be impossible within these limits to attempt any description of Decker's effects. The last part of the book, not often found complete with the rest, deals with gardens and finishes this epitome of what wealth could do.

The same firm of publishers gave to the world the most beautiful theatrical book ever printed, the *Theatralische Tanzschüle* of Gregorio Lambranzi. This amazing study of dancing extends to two volumes of fifty plates each, and has an explanation of each dance in German and Italian. Lambranzi was a Venetian who became Court chorographer to the Elector of Bavaria ; his book was published in 1716 when he was an old man, and we may assume that it contains the whole fruits of his lifetime of invention and experience. I give a couple of illustrations that will show the strength and poetical fullness of this dancer's fancy ; the frontispiece to the second volume, in which the author is seen as Mezzetin, will draw tears to the eyes when the present state of theatrical art is remembered by contrast.

I have mentioned this book because the recently discovered theatrical drawings and costumes that were found and shown to the public for the first time after the War, when they had lain unnoticed for years in the Hofbibliothek of Vienna, give convincing proof that the period of Leopold I. was the Golden Age of theatrical production—that is to say, the Periclean and Shakespearian ages have their counterpart in this period of supreme representation. A whole new race of artists have come to light, and their works, that are now in course of publication in the Viennese series called "Monumenta Scenica," go far towards explaining the Baroque splendours of Germany. With this newly found knowledge we can see in the light of such men as Ottaviano Burnacini, or the Bibbiena family, exactly how and why it was that Fischer von Erlach or Lukas von Hildebrandt was so swift and easy in his effects — how, to use a colloquialism—he got it across the footlights with such conspicuous freedom and brilliance. Good technique finds its justification in their achievement and we begin to expect of architects of the second order that they should be supremely competent, if not exactly inspired.

There are other books that we can invoke as witness—for instance, the work on the Zwinger palace by Poeppelmann, or Salomon Kleiner's prints of the Orangery of Prince Eugene at the Belvedere with its menagerie and aviary. As the books get smaller in scale they do not lose any of their verbal redundancy, and the almanacs of the day are so heavily strewn with titles that it is painful to turn the pages. The German Princes of the Empire, the Bans of Croatia, the Magnates of Hungary, the Nobles of Bohemia, the Transylvanian Barons, a

Hospodar or two—these move thickly through the pages, or appear in the books of views as the owners of such or such a Viennese palace. Then there are the Knights of the Golden Fleece and of the Teutonic Order, the latter body, I may say, being responsible for many fine eighteenth-century buildings in Germany and Bohemia.

We may establish Vienna, then, as the centre of the whole of this world of mediæval survival, and the working ground of the best architects of the day. Fischer von Erlach and Lukas von Hildebrandt, the two architects of Vienna, had a fluency and copiousness that was truly extraordinary. Moreover they were concerned with great cities, and are for that reason alone a safe guide to modern practitioners of the same craft. They possessed, also, a lightness that we have been taught never to associate with the Teuton at work. As a matter of fact, the German buildings of this period are, beyond question, the best of their date, and no other country can show work of the same age that is so successful in the solution of all its problems. Vienna has more, and better, palaces of the kind than are to be seen in Rome, and the few still existing gardens are unique in their kind. Vienna is the only big city of that day with a commensurate building activity which can still be studied. Bath, Nancy, and Rennes, are perhaps the only other towns that are in the least inspiring as examples of what a town could and should be, but for some reason people who are loud in their clamouring for what they conceive to be modernity so often select out of the past for their admiration, and to act as model, Stonehenge and the Stone Age, Maori houses, Peruvian tomb mounds, very strict and very early East Anglian Gothic, or anything and everything that is inappropriate to their purpose.

The canons of exuberance that were first formulated by

Bernini we can see carried a step further in this metropolis of anti-democracy, and their victories over the Turks joined with the ancient feudal German position of the Hapsburgs and their legendary Imperial Roman station gave a superb excuse for this self-justified magnificence. In the foreground, as I have hinted, we may place Slovaks and Bohemians, the Hussars of Hungary, Pandours, Morlacchi, Croats, and all the rest of the auxiliary Bashi Bazouks of the day, with, later on, the fiercely moustached warriors of Poland, and, yet later still, the Gondoliers and Patricians of Venice. It is like a list of costume designs, or an account of an Indian Durbar. Is it to be wondered at that the Pope treated the Emperor with an obsequiousness that the number of churches and convents in his dominions made excusable? Of the three children of that perpetual embodiment and mystical paternity, the Papacy, the Holy Roman Emperor was the chosen one, and the Kings of France and Spain were treated with a kindliness not tinged with so much favouritism. Of course the fact that the Duchy of Tuscany became, by 1740, an appanage of the Austrian Crown was not without weight upon this attitude, for Austria, which historians always try to represent as weak, was actually the strongest European Power in the time of Prince Eugene, and even Frederick the Great did not dare humble her to too deep an extent. She was, all through that century, as powerful in Italy as in Germany, with Savoy like a kind of weak Prussia upon her flank.

We wish that it were possible to reproduce here some of the portraits with which German books upon our period are illustrated, so that our readers might know the appearance of such military heroes as Prince Henry of Prussia or General von Ziethen. Without such auxiliaries it is difficult to conjure up the martinet, that character with which eighteenth-century Germany was so thickly populated. Nor is it possible to represent adequately the unthinkable slavery to which the subjects of Prussia or Hesse were condemned in the form of military service. The whole hideous frame of this discipline was founded upon corporal punishment, and one is left in the end with nothing but contempt for a race that could endure it without revolt. These strange, sadistic military types can be seen portrayed in a formula that gives relief to their essentially beastly countenances, and it is a world of perpetual public execution, or of wretched deserters running the gauntlet.

The pleasant alternative to this hopelessness is the German music of the time, and it may perhaps help to explain the excellence of architecture in these lands at this period in the same way that the quantities of Elizabethan music recently unearthed help one to understand how that extraordinary body of poetry was created. There is a kind of solid inspiration about some of these façades that makes one think of the diurnal cantatas or motets turned out regularly by the great musicians of the day. One would like to know details of the digestive system of a man like Fischer von Erlach, whose work shows practically no signs of "seediness," and one has an identical curiosity as to the details of Bach's life, for these data are of immense importance and give, perhaps, the key to a whole lifework.

This sifted Italianism, refined through the rather large meshes of a German understanding of detail—for there ought from their point of view always to be too much ornament, and that executed too minutely—has, in Central Europe, become mellowed by a less exacting climatic condition, for there is not the parched summer of Rome or Sicily to be guarded against. Indeed, the Danube Valley we may consider as an almost ideal mean between the extremes of North and South, and the same with regard to Southern Bavaria. The orchards are of apple, not orange, and the artificial condition that this latter fruit demands for its ripening away from Sicily or Rome has been converted into an excuse for inventing some of the most beautiful of architectural effects in the Orangeries that they erected. The Baroque has become the true national expression of this part of the world, and many streets in Dresden and many small isolated houses in towns like Bamberg show that these canons were applicable to buildings less proud than palace or convent. The innumerable small courts all over the German-speaking world were as prodigal in their magnificence as any small Italian duchy, and either Ansbach or Wörlitz is a more harmonious whole than Modena or Turin, even if it does not possess the picture galleries for which these towns are famous. One day the century between 1650 and 1750 will be recognised as a period in which every detail of workmanship was more perfect than at any other time save the twelfth century, when the mediæval world was growing into ripeness. It may not be great art, but it is small art at perfection, and this age was at its best flowering in Central Europe.

Those two great river valleys, the Rhine and the Danube, had their mediæval romanticism of castle or ruin enlarged by the new abbey or Elector's villa rising from their banks. The old became completed by the new and formed that true harmony of which modern art is afraid, for it never realises that the new always enhances the old, so long, that is to say, as it is really new and typical of the date, not merely an archæological revival. The toothed and prickly mediæval ornament becomes rounded and curving, less difficult to catch your foot in, less of an excrescence and more a part of the building. If they had tried a "revival" we should have St Pancras Station or Keble College where Melk and Göttweig now stand on their cliffs above the

Danube, but they were self-confident and did not suffer from any reticence or complex of inferiority. We are left, as a result of this optimism, with two of the finest conscious buildings in Europe, and that kind of triumph of the imagination which we can conceive carried into execution by a man of the originality and genius of Vanbrugh. We may picture that great artist transferred from England to Austria and employed there on a series of great undertakings which were not curtailed or interfered with, and which had a public character either as convents or palaces occurring in the midst of a large town, so that they entered in some degree into the lives of the population and were not entirely hidden away in the depths of a park. Such are some of the palaces of Prague and Vienna, and we must people them with the retinue suitable to persons of such territorial importance as the Esterházy or the Liechtenstein family, who owned estates in Bohemia that stretched for two hundred miles to the frontiers of Silesia, while both families maintained their own private regiments of grenadiers and hussars.

Many particularities and much divergence must be taken into account when it is realised that down to the French Revolution the German Empire consisted of more than three hundred distinct states, while even the relics of this feudal system, when they were repaired after the fall of Napoleon and the German Confederation was formed, could not be reduced to a lower number than thirty-eight independent states, at which figure it remained, more or less, till the European War. Freak princes and petty absurdities flourished in this soil as nowhere else, which fortunate flowering makes a great deal of the interest that this period instils in any mind that is interested in the effect of environment upon personality. It becomes in the mind a kind of restful paradise of intrigue after the horror of the world as

26

demonstrated through such mouthpieces as " Pertinax " or Captain Bruce Bairnsfather.

Architects such as Fischer von Erlach, Lukas von Hildebrandt, Kilian Ignaz Dientzenhofer, and J. B. Neumann become construed into personalities, for they are more the property of the public by their achievement than men like William Kent or Vanbrugh. In certain effects they are supreme : there have never been such magnificent staircases as at the Belvedere, at Würzburg, at Brühl, or at Schloss Pommersfelden ; there have never been such wrought-iron gates as at Potsdam, Würzburg, or the Abbey of Zwiefalten ; and French taste seems always mean compared to German, while Italian work of the day suffers, save at Caserta, from an enforced economy, so that it looks shoddy and cheaply finished. This is the chief drawback to the beautiful Venetian furniture of that day, for the workmanship is always poor compared to the delicacy of the design. The Germans were prepared to spend much longer over their work than the Italians, and if they completed it with as much detail as the French they had at any rate designed it at the outset from a larger point of view. It is, therefore, of more masculine conception than French work ; but while it has this one feature of English design it has not the English reticence, or, if another name is preferred, self-consciousness. Nor was German taste obsessed by the principles of Palladianism, which severe canons held back and too strictly regulated the native fantasy of our architects. However admirable may be the interiors of Kent or Adams it must be confessed that their façades are a little depressing in their strictness, for the cold exterior is almost too reliant upon good breeding and the enforcement of good manners. In fact, it recalls that national embodiment Mr Chester Coote in Mr Wells' novel, *Kipps*.

Many persons have a weakness for those suspiciously sharp-

27

edged water-colours of Albert Dürer, and it must be at once conceded that this rather debatable artistic figure is most certainly to be preferred in this medium. A little way behind him are Altdorfer, Sebald Beham, and a host of others, while Breughel has by now come to be considered as a German master, because his pictures are to be seen in any quantity only in Vienna. However typically Flemish he may be, he at any rate painted the hilly and half-Alpine landscape that lies on the borders of Switzerland and is inhabited by a polyglot population that speak German as well as they can any other language, while his pictures partake of that Central European character which we find expressed in the water-colours I have just mentioned.

These high, pointed hills thickly clad with fir-trees, the mediæval castle on the summit, the thin air smelling of fir-cone and bonfire, the apple-orchard below, the walled gardens hung with apricots, the small apple-green mountain lakes, rye bread, and white wines from the Rhine provinces — these are the substitutes that we must produce for cypress avenues, white oxen, and thickly strewn remnants of classical sculpture as they occur in the pictures of every artist who has ever been to Rome. In this more suitable context the German buildings of that day look born to their environment. They have made a brave show of classical descent and protected their claims with a fine flourish of heraldic fable. The Northern and Gothic wilderness has given birth to something that is anxious to make greater claims—as though there were a buried treasure hidden somewhere in the pine woods. It is this peculiar and natural flowing of mediævalism into more direct channels that we are studying, and this classical pretension seems fresher and more original from long absence. The whole world seems disposed for the preservation of those long pointed chins of the Hapsburgs, and the Holy Roman

Emperors have existed for so long—ever since the time of Charlemagne—that their hereditary right from the first Rudolph must be supported at whatever cost to the race. The Electors, the Margraves, and the Prince Bishops were fully agreed as to this, for in the days of which we are treating, the Hapsburgs had already secured this honour for a permanence of three centuries. They all, in fact, depended upon each other, and the people thought they depended upon them. Even now they seem uncertain whether they do, or do not. We will not pretend to depend upon their architects, but the study of their works may be useful.

II

An Architectural Tour

THE range of date with which this book is concerned treats of the German hegemony under the presidency of but two Emperors—Leopold I. and Charles VI. We must, therefore, familiarise ourselves with their appearance, for the heraldic Hapsburg features which were so palpable in them are as often recognised in the art of the period as is the W.L., entwined, by which the Compagnie des Wagons-Lits asserts its sway on a thousand European expresses. Leopold I. then, the implacable and proudly unconcerned router of the Turks, who refused his hand to Sobieski after the victory of Vienna—what was he like? In Plate XXV of this book he may be seen in an ivory statuette, where he is represented trampling a Turk under his horse's hoofs. He is armour-clad, holds a marshal's baton, and is checking his Spanish barb so that the cloak flutters out behind him with the violence of his arrested motion. The Turk, it may be noted, has thrown up his right leg in self-defence so that the foot strikes against the belly of the Emperor's horse and serves at the same time to bolster up the perilous ivory pose. The Emperor is laurel-crowned over his periwig, and is, so far as features go, almost the precise counterpart of a contemporary European King who, in 1926, was waging war with an army of one hundred and fifty thousand men against the Moors.

Leopold is always represented in a whirl of victory—seen perhaps to his greatest advantage in that extraordinary saloon painted by Fra Pozzo in the Bishop's Palace at Bamberg, where he appears out of a flame-coloured wall, niched as though he was a statue, in a great periwig, and further intensified by a fierce warrior's moustaches.

His successor, Charles VI. — the last male Hapsburg — is shown here in two portraits. The first of these is a print by G. A. Müller after the portrait painted in 1730 by Jacob van Schuppen. He is shown in the robes of the Order of the Golden Fleece, and is seated, to all appearances uncomfortably, while his elbow rests on a heavy table which is loaded with cushions and with the glittering overflow of both his robe and the great curtain draped above him. His feet are on a tasselled cushion, and the whole of this pomp is raised on a dais of two steps, which is covered with a golden cloth that ripples down, like water, on to the marble pavement of the hall. In the background there is a kind of painted drop with rich architectural accessory of pillar and portico, altogether like a Bibbiena "set." The second portrait of him which we reproduce here is by the Neapolitan painter, Francesco Solimena. It shows Count Althann heavily kneeling in periwig and breastplate, while, with an appearance of grace that it must have been difficult to assume, he hands to the Emperor the catalogue of the picture gallery in the Belvedere. There are two celestial bodies above Charles manœuvring themselves so as to place a wreath upon his forehead, and behind the Emperor, to either side of him, are two young pages in attendance upon him. The Emperor is in full armour, and two halberdiers in the background fill the left corner and complete the composition, though a very peaceful little dog barking at the Count diminishes the martial ardour of the scene. There are no Turks—it was considered that by this time they were negligible, thanks to Prince Eugene.

We come now to that great General's apotheosis, carved in a huge block of marble and to be seen in the recently opened Baroque Museum in the Lower Belvedere at Vienna. It represents him in full armour, struggling against his foes, and trampling them under his feet, while Fame and Victory and a number of other personifications all struggle for a footing upon the small marble base of the group. It is an apotheosis for once deserved because Prince Eugene was a person of such importance that it is no exaggeration to say he disposed of the whole of the eighteenth century as regards Central Europe, and that but for him the Austrian Empire would have never survived till the end of the European War. In fact Prince Eugene and Frederick the Great are the two outstanding political figures of the eighteenth century. Prince Eugene, the reputed son of Louis XIV., had in any case a suspicious love of magnificence, for he built the two finest palaces of the eighteenth century in Vienna—the Belvedere and the former Winter Palace. This deserved tribute, then, is his just due. The sculptor was Balthasar Permoser (1651-1732), who worked chiefly in Dresden after a prolonged studentship in Italy, and finished this particular group in 1721. He worked in Berlin from 1704 to 1710 for the Elector Frederick I., and his chief works in Dresden include the pulpit in the Hofkirche, some of the sculptures at the Zwinger Palace, and the *Apotheosis of Augustus the Strong*. He was also an excellent carver in ivory, and there is an excellent ivory group of Hercules and Omphale by him in the Schloss Museum at Berlin.

With these three names, Leopold I., Charles VI., and Prince Eugene, we are principally concerned, for they were the patrons of all the art of their day, and we must detail their patronage and mention the talent they employed upon their works. The two great architects of Vienna were Johann Bernhardt Fischer von

Erlach and Johann Lukas von Hildebrandt; it is to these two men that Vienna owes her character as a city, and this is true of them to a greater extent than it can be said of Bernini with regard to Rome.

Johann Bernhardt Fischer von Erlach was born at Graz in 1656. His first work in Vienna after returning from his studentship in Italy was the execution of the Trinity Column in the Graben, from a sketch by Ottaviano Burnacini. This is a remarkable piece of pose and equilibrium, comparable to the guglia of Southern Italy and Naples. We shall see later on in these pages that such queer pieces of religious symbolism were popular in Silesia, that far-away province of the Empire where seventeenth-century work shows close affinities to the Spanish "excesses" of the same period. The Trinity Column was started in 1687 and finished in 1693, and the fact that its designer, Burnacini, was the great stage-artist of the day is indicative of the atmosphere in which this strange project of cloud-shapes rendered into stone was conceived. Burnacini is known to us, besides this, by a selection, published in the series "Monumenta Scenica," from a great folio of miniature paintings of costumes that he executed in his old age for the Emperor Leopold I., making a kind of idealised *résumé* of what he had seen and of what he considered possible in the way of stage-dress. Some of his architectural designs for operas and ballets have been reproduced in another volume of the same series and show this forgotten genius working in the manner of Ferdinando Galli Bibbiena.

The execution of the Trinity Column from a design of Burnacini was, then, the first big work entrusted to Fischer von Erlach. At the same time, in order to obtain a complete mastery over his subject, he was working in the Belvedere under a fresco-painter called Louis Dorigny, who was painting decorations for Prince Eugene. After the Trinity Column Fischer was engaged for some years on various buildings in Salzburg, beginning with the principal doorway to the Hofstalle-Kaserne, and culminating in 1696 with the University church, his first really important structure, with a dome, two towers, and a projecting semicircular façade of three storeys reaching nearly to the parapets of the towers on each side. This projecting porch, as it were, is reminiscent of the Carignano palace in Turin, the work of Guarino Guarini, and, in fact, the whole of this first church of Fischer's is permeated, not so much with the true Roman Baroque, as with the slight and poor feats that were all Borromini had ever the commissions to execute seen in a larger scale through the big accomplishment of Guarini in Turin. In the interior the chief altar is rayed and clouded in white and gold in that manner invented by Bernini for St Peter's, and two windows, a tall oblong and an oval above it, throw light upon this drift of clouds that is broken with gilded sun-rays and has flights of angels coming through its intervals. The church of Holy Trinity is much less interesting; it is domed and has two towers and, this time, a recessed semicircular façade, but it is carried out in a dry and flat manner about which it is difficult to feel interest. St John's Hospital is an improvement upon this, but neither of these churches bears comparison with the University church.

From about 1696 Fischer entered upon his true career of success and it is pleasant to find him turning from church to palace architecture. In that year he drew the first plans for Schönbrunn, but work was only started some twenty years later, and in its present state Schönbrunn has nothing of Fischer about it. The Schwarzenberg Palace in Vienna was his next important work and this in its central feature recalls the projecting porch of the University church. It is, however, an uninteresting façade and not by any means a good example of Fischer's power. In these years he made the garden to the Liechtenstein Palace, a building by the Italian Domenico Martinelli, and completed it with a magnificent doorway of Atlantes and a finely imagined coat of arms posed by a couple of cupids in front of the balcony and between two conventional stone vases on pilasters. Besides this, he made a belvedere for the end of the garden, but this was unfortunately destroyed many years ago.

Immediately following upon this we find Fischer in 1701 at work upon one of his most typical buildings, the Schönborn, formerly Batthyany Palace in the Renngasse. It is of no great size, but these Hungarian Magnates were put by Fischer into a house that contained strangely inappropriate and strictly Roman-looking reliefs in every blank above the windows of the first floor. The doorway is of an exceptionally sober design, compensated by the huge crown and the heraldic sculptures above the window over the entrance. The pilasters, of a strange and flat order, rise up from this first floor into the storey above and break into disproportionate and voluted capitals.

Fischer was now working for Prince Eugene upon his Winter Palace, one of the two great buildings that went by his name, the other being the Belvedere, the Prince's Summer Palace. It is now the Reichs-Finanz-Ministerium, and it was built between 1703 and 1711 by the combined talents of Fischer von Erlach and Lukas von Hildebrandt. The façade has received special treatment on account of its facing such a narrow street; it is, therefore, arranged with more care for its lateral appearance, as it was generally to be seen sideways as you walked down its length towards the doorway. There are three nearly similar doorways each crowned with a balcony, and an heraldic achievement and crown, above the first-floor window. The interior-staircase is magnificent, and makes a really fine specimen of stair-treatment as it is to be seen in German palace and monastery.

After about 1707 Fischer's output of work became so great that he had to leave the details of a great many of his buildings to his son, Josef Emanuel. The Clam-Gallas Palace at Prague dates from about this period, and the two end-pavilions of the façade are treated in a peculiar manner above the tremendously sculptured doorways, each with two pairs of Atlantes upholding the plinths of a heavy balcony. In 1714 the Böhmischen Hofkanzlei, now the Ministry of the Interior, was finished, and this possesses the most magnificent of all Fischer's doorways. The entrance, instead of being confined architecturally to one window-width, is spread out over three, and there is a grilled window on each side of the doorway, while the whole design is carried up upon the shoulders of four caryatid-terms past four statues that guard the chief window with its balcony and the windows on either side of it into a huge capping of cloud-shapes and heraldry above the three windows together.

Before dealing with Fischer's last and greatest works we will summarise his lesser achievements that have not so far been noticed. These include the palace of Prince Auersperg, which was begun by him in 1722 for the Marchese di Roffrano, the Auersperg family having purchased it only in 1776; and the palace of Prince Trautson, built from his designs between 1720 and 1730, which was purchased by the Government in 1760 and handed over to be the residence of the Hungarian Noble Guard. This latter is one of his most successful works. The windows above the entrance have keystones to their arches that have been worked into plumed helmets and the balcony above these prophecies of war is decorated with two fine stone groups

36

of a couple of figures each. The three windows of the first floor are crowned with heavy mouldings that support seated figures. Inside, there is a magnificent staircase rising between a pair of stone sphinxes and a couple of Atlantes ; but the beauty of this palace is much diminished by the absence of that magnificent uniform which I described a few pages back. Apart from Vienna, Fischer built, as I have said, the Clam-Gallas Palace at Prague, three churches at Salzburg, and the oval hall of the ancestors and the circular church at Schloss Frain, Wranau, near Brünn in Moravia.

But Fischer's fame rests upon two works, the Karlskirche and part of the Hofburg at Vienna. The Karlskirche was started in 1715 as a thank-offering for the cessation of the plague, and was eventually finished in 1737. Two tall domed belfries at either side have most of their hundred feet of height covered with reliefs in the manner of Trajan's Column, which carvings, by the sculptors Mader and Schletter, tell the achievements, more moral than material, of San Carlo Borromeo. These two belfries make a fine contrast with the dome and recall inevitably the effects obtained in Persia with the minarets and the domed mosques. The dome of the Karlskirche is a remarkably fine specimen of its class and is carried on eight piers between four great and four lesser openings. The corner towers of the church which frame these two belfries complete the whole composition of dome, façade, and towers. The interior of the church, over which we may assume that Fischer had but little control, is remarkable for its fine marbles and for the pulpits and the choir-boxes more theatrical than sacred.

We now arrive at the final and most famous achievement of Fischer's secular career, the Hofburg. In this case, as in that of the Karlskirche, Charles VI. was the patron to whom everything was due. Unfortunately the commission came late in Fischer's life and he did not live to see more than a mere fraction of his plans carried out, though they were completed in portion by his son, Josef Emanuel, who died in 1742. Actually, the Winter Riding School, the inner façade of the Reichskanzlei, and the Hofbibliothek, are the only buildings for which the Fischers can be held responsible, in the sense that they were alive and able to superintend and supervise. The Winter Riding School, for instance, was built in 1729-1735 by the son from his father's designs, when the latter had already been dead some ten years. The Reichskanzlei was finished in 1728, and here the Council of the Empire held their deliberations in the eighteenth century, though in later times it became the residence of that discomfort-loving old autocrat, Franz-Josef. The Hofbibliothek is by far the finest of these three, and altogether the finest achievement of Fischer's life. Great staircases lead up to the library hall above, which has a frescoed dome painted by Daniel Gran, and magnificently carved bookcases, the higher tiers of which are reached by twisting stairways and a walnut gallery. This is the finest library design in the world, and the only thing I have ever seen to approach it, though this does so only in the elegance of its detail and by no means in boldness or originality of planning, is the library of red and green lacquer in the University at Coimbra in Portugal.

The Hofbibliothek is the centre-block of three sides of a square, the right-hand wing being the Ballroom and the Spanish Riding School, while the left wing contains a number of smaller apartments. These three sides of a square have been treated as a whole, being a rusticated ground storey with Ionic pilasters running through two floors above this. The material is stucco, and the whole exterior design may be, perhaps, too dry and staid.

The Reichskanzlei forms another whole wing of the Hofburg, but this is an unbroken and emphatic façade crowned with many trophies of arms, with eagles with outstretched wings, and with figures blowing trumpets. It cannot be compared favourably, though, with the Consulta, the palace built next to the Quirinal for the Pope's Lifeguards by Ferdinando Fuga (1699-1780), for here the design is more free and digested, the statues stand more easily upon the roof-line, and there is a much greater mobility and freedom. Here, then, the German is inferior to the Roman work of the eighteenth century.

Fischer's plans for the whole lay-out of the Hofburg were to a great extent carried out towards the end of last century, so that, although in its details the work is conspicuously that of 1870 to 1890, the conception and the planning have Fischer's feeling behind them, and the whole group of the Hofburg may be judged in its entirety as representative of this great architect's work.

His last piece of invention was the fountain for the Hoher Markt, a most delightful conception based upon the design of a baldachino. Very soon after this Fischer von Erlach died, on the 5th April 1723; he was only sixty-seven years old. Two years before his death, in 1721, he published his *Entwürf einer historischen Architektur*; this was again reprinted at Leipzig in 1725, and in 1737 an English edition was published by Thomas Lediard, who had been a secretary in the English Embassy at Vienna. The book is divided into five sections dealing with the whole history of architecture, but the fourth section, which contains a selection from Fischer's own designs, is naturally the most interesting part of the book. Here can be seen the whole of Fischer's elaborate and never executed designs for Schönbrunn which he conceived as an elaborate fantasy in the vein of Paulus Decker the Elder. The designs of such palaces as these are the absolute culmination of the aristocratic principle, where the prince would be living in the middle of his Court surrounded by his lifeguards, with the whole of nature cut and trimmed into alleys and parterres for his diversion. In Germany, artists of the wildest fancy found their dreams materialised into fact, as we shall see in many places that this book describes. Fischer von Erlach was comparatively a strict and regular practician compared with some of the amazing effects arrived at in the more remote parts of Germany, where a Margrave or a Prince Bishop held absolute dominion and the whole of life was not regulated and made a little ordinary by the presence of the machinery of Government on a scale like that made necessary by the size of the Hapsburg dominions.

A near rival, if not an equal to Fischer, was the other great architect of Vienna, Johann Lukas von Hildebrandt. He was born at Genoa in 1666 and lived to the age of seventy-nine, dying in 1745. He worked at Prague nearly as much as at Vienna and was altogether more of a private architect; he did little or no Government work, and very few churches are to his credit. His masterpiece is the Belvedere, or Summer Palace of Prince Eugene in Vienna. It was begun in 1713, and the Lower Belvedere,[1] with the stables, was completed and occupied by the Prince in 1716. The garden stretching between the two palaces was started the next year by the Bavarian garden-architect, Girard, and is one of the most beautiful urban gardens in existence, with its flights of steps, statues, and high clipped hedges. The Upper Belvedere has a great sheet of water in front of it, round the edges of which you have to walk in order to reach the palace, once you have passed through and under

[1] In this Lower Belvedere the Baroque Museum of Vienna has been installed. It is a unique collection in a miraculously beautiful setting.

the magnificent iron-grilled gates of entrance. The hall from which the great stair starts has caryatid pillars, most of them bulky, bearded men bowed under their loads, for the plinths that they carry, out of which the vaults of the ceiling spring forth, are heavily festooned with trumpet, drum, and spear. Between them, through the central alley, you can see the garden stretching away down to the Lower Belvedere. The great stair starts up from here, which, even in the photograph reproduced, shows something of the flashing, snowy whiteness of its effect. This is one of the four great staircases of Germany, the others being at Schloss Pommersfelden, Brühl, and Würzburg. The upper rooms of the palace are decorated from the designs of Claudius le Fort du Plessy, and have, besides their boiseried walls and stuccoed ceilings, the most beautiful views from the windows over the garden.

Lukas von Hildebrandt was employed with Fischer, as we have seen, upon the Winter Palace of Prince Eugene. Besides this, he built the Kinsky Palace between 1709 and 1713 for Count Daun, the celebrated Field-Marshal. He worked, also, at Prague, but this is better described when Prague is reached in the course of our itinerary.

Before we leave Vienna we must mention the work of several other architects mainly of Italian origin who worked in the city. The Breuner Palace, with one of the finest façades in Vienna, has two great groups of Hercules and Antæus, Æneas and Anchises, adorning its exterior, and in default of any precise information I would suggest that it may have been designed by a Milanese architect, for it resembles many buildings, notably the Palazzo Litta, in that city. The best Italian architect practising in Vienna was Domenico Martinelli of Lucca, who built (1701–1712) the old Summer Palace of Prince Liechtenstein, the garden and façade of which are familiar to all students of Italian eighteenth-century painters by the two magnificent pictures by Bellotto still in the Liechtenstein collection. The rooms in which the famous picture gallery is housed are superb examples of the best work of the period, with rich stucco decorations and ceiling paintings by Belluzzi, Pozzo and Franceschini, the last named of these having been a pupil of Gio. Battista Galli Bibbiena and having had the reputation of being the foremost perspectivist of his day. The town-palace of Prince Liechtenstein is also from the designs of Dom. Martinelli, aided in this instance by Gabrielli of Rovereto. Other works by Martinelli are the Schloss at Austerlitz, and the monastery of Hradisch, near Olmütz in Bohemia.

Compared with the number of palaces in Vienna, there are few churches of our period that have much interest. Besides the Karlskirche, attention should be drawn to the Old University church, rebuilt about 1705 and decorated with frescoes by the great perspectivist, Fratel Pozzo, who was summoned from Rome soon after he had finished his frescoes in S. Ignazio by Prince Liechtenstein. Pozzo helped to decorate the Summer Palace of that family and his influence upon the school of Viennese decorative painters was most pronounced. While living in Vienna Pozzo painted the high-altarpiece and the six side-altarpieces in the University church, the high-altar of the Franciscan church, and some pictures for the Dominican church. He died at Vienna in 1709. The Peterskirche, perhaps wrongly ascribed to Fischer von Erlach, is a good baroque structure, and the ceiling of its choir, as well as one or two of its nine altarpieces, are " by Bibbiena," though I have been unable to find out which member of this gifted family is referred to in that phrase. We may mention, also, the Salesian Nunnery built probably by Fischer von Erlach ; the church of St Anna built for the Jesuits and frescoed in 1747 by Daniel Gran, the decorator of the Hofbibliothek ; and the church of the Savoyard nuns in the Johannesgasse, where the stucco-work is of an amazing excellence.

The château of Schönbrunn, just outside Vienna, is the most delightful example imaginable of a summer palace. The huge plans that were made for it by J. B. Fischer von Erlach, which are illustrated in the book that he published, were hardly begun, and work at the château was resumed in 1744 by Maria Theresa under the direction of an Italian, Niccolo Pacassi. It contains the most enchanting mirror- and tapestry-rooms, and has good ceilings by Gregorio Guglielmi. The gardens still have the old clipped hedges, some thirty feet in height, and the garden sculptures are by an excellent artist, J. W. Beyer, who died in 1806, and even in a few instances by the great Raphael Donner. There is another interesting Imperial Palace at Laxenburg, outside Vienna, but only a few good rooms of our period are left, and the old classical garden has been ruined and transformed into an English landscape-garden. There is nothing, therefore, at Laxenburg which at all compares in interest or beauty with Schönbrunn.

In order to conclude *the* actual Kingdom of Austria there remain to be described the great monasteries on the Danube, which are the chief architectural feature of that country-side. The four principal of these *are*, Klosterneuburg, Melk, Göttweig, and St Florian. The first of these, an Augustinian abbey, is some ten or twelve miles from Vienna, on the right bank of the river. The building, which was originally twelfth-century work, in the far from first-rate Gothic of these regions, was rebuilt in its present form between 1689 and 1714, though the Gothic cloisters are still intact by the church. The actual

43

residential part of the abbey was rebuilt in 1730-1750 by an Italian named Felice Donato d'Allio, and it was the intention of the Emperor Charles VI. to build a huge palace for himself in the abbey precincts—an ambition that he only partially fulfilled; but even that fragment has an air of great magnificence with its staircase, marble saloon, and suite of rooms hung with fine tapestries. The ducal bonnet of the Regents of Austria, with which the Emperor is crowned on his accession, is kept in this monastery, to which it was entrusted by the Emperor Maximilian, and a wrought-iron version appears above the east dome of the monastery buildings, the west dome being ornamented with an immense Imperial crown. The chief revenue of this monastery was formerly derived, as was the case with most of these monasteries, from the sale of Klosterneuburg wine, the produce of vineyards belonging to the monks.

Going up the Danube towards Bavaria, the next convent reached is Melk, some forty miles from Vienna, which stands in a magnificent position on a cliff some two hundred feet above the river. It was rebuilt, between 1707 and 1736, by an architect from St Polten named Jakob Prandtauer, a local practitioner with the most grandiose of talents. In this one work, indeed, Prandtauer shows himself the equal of either of the more re-nowned architects we have been discussing. The Benedictine Abbey of Melk is the biggest in all the German lands, and this quality of size is made use of in the most effective manner, for the architect's virtuosity has placed the entrance to the church between the two towers of the convent, with an open colonnade in front that looks out over the Danube valley. From this colonnaded walk the two lateral wings stretch away in the two directions of the river-bed and their hundreds of windows in that flashing white of the two façades make a sight that will never be forgotten by anyone interested in this last of European architectures. The church has splendid marbles and the most richly carved stalls and pulpits; there are the usual Abbot's apartments and Königsaal with tiled stoves, portraits, and tapestries, and, last of all, there is the library, which is decorated in blue and gold and nearly rivals the Hofbibliothek of Vienna. In all, this monastery of Melk is one of the wonders of the eighteenth century and is the first specimen we have yet had occasion to mention in this book of a great class of monasteries, the last great product of the monastic principles. There are some half-dozen of these in Austria, and about the like number in Bavaria.

Göttweig, the second of these, is another Benedictine monastery, and only some few miles north of Melk. It covers the top of a hill of some seven hundred feet about four miles from the Danube. It was rebuilt at exactly the same period as Melk, and is of positively colossal dimensions. It has a magnificent staircase with a great ceiling painted by Paul Troger, and the usual church, sacristies, library, Kaisersaal, and Abbot's apartments that would be expected of its size and importance.

The Augustinian abbey of St Florian, which is higher up the Danube towards Linz, is no less remarkable than the two already mentioned. The buildings were designed by Prandtauer and by three members, Bartolommeo, Diego, and Carlo Antonio, of the Genoese family of Carlone who produced a regular succession of architects, painters, and sculptors, for some four generations. This monastery is of a more compact plan than that at Melk; it rises in a huge, square mass above the market-place of the town; the church with its two towers is in the midst of this square, and on the other side the usual Königsaal projects for another two storeys above the ordinary façade and is emphasised by decisive pilasters that rise up and break into their capitals just below the attic storey. The gate of the monastery, by Carlone, is a more than usually ambitious affair occupying three floors, beginning on each side of the door with a pair of Atlantes and continuing with two more couples of figures flanking the balcony, with a pair of terms supporting yet another balcony, and with the cornice of the window above this ridden by two cupids trumpeting fame into the capitals of the columns of the façade that are just breaking at this point below the ordinary level of the cornice into their Corinthian heads. The other side of the court to which this is the entrance contains the great staircase of the monastery, a double affair running up in two flights, with three open and unglazed windows to each length of its four reaches. The staircase block is, therefore, of six bays, with a great window in the middle, these intervals being marked by seven Corinthian pillars. The church of St Florian has its roof and dome painted in the most skilful manner of theatrical perspective ; and the rococo stalls and organ, and the presses for vestments in the sacristy with their plain panels and rich rococo cresting, where cupids are climbing among the carved garlands near to the painted and coved sacristy ceiling, all of these things have reached to a pitch of excellence that the baroque never attained to in Italy or Spain. The great stairway has fine wrought-iron gates to defend its flights, and the balustrade of the landing above is ornamented with vases and groups of cupids and with a stuccoed and painted ceiling, making a suitable prelude to the Königsaal, or Marmorsaal, a huge vaulted room with ceiling of elaborate perspective and two giant mantelpieces covered with heraldic achievement, the work of the Carloni. A magnificent suite of rooms opens from here, a room frescoed with hunting-scenes, an audience-hall with huge carved chimney-piece, also by the Carloni, a tapestry-room, and another painted room with a most extraordinary gilded and rococo bed that can be ascribed without hesitation to the Carloni. A library and a painted refectory complete this extravagant epitome of monastic life.

Another great Benedictine abbey, that of Kremsmünster, lies not many miles from St Florian, near the town of Wels. This has five cloisters, and an observatory eight storeys high, containing on its lower floors a collection of paintings and antiquities. There are several unusual and remarkable features about this monastery. To begin with, some sculptor of peculiar fancy has placed over the entrance arch three statues, the central one being of the founder, Duke Tassilo of Bavaria, who accomplished this pious deed in the year 777. His two companions and himself are of giant and robust vigour, looking like Vikings or Wagnerian heroes, in plate armour with capes of ermine, and full-blooded *landsknecht* beards below the most florid of crowns, all three of these heads being thrown into relief against as many recessed white shells in the wall. The church, the library, the refectory, the Kaisersaal, and the usual tapestry-rooms, we might describe as ordinary specimens of this magnificence, but one monkish peculiarity has here been carried to its extreme limit. This consists of five tanks of fish-preserves, each kept under lock and key, and each decorated with colonnades and fine fountain-statues of saints, huntsmen, fishermen, or tritons who ride their dolphins and sound their conch-shells or grasp their tridents fiercely in alarm. Unfortunately, even while these lines are being written, it has been announced in the papers that the monks have been forced from poverty to sell their famous " Flemish Espalier " tapestries to the Metropolitan Museum of New York.

To conclude this class of building, we may mention another Benedictine monastery, that of Seitenstetten, some twenty-five miles from Linz. Church, staircase, Marmorsaal, tapestry-rooms, library, and refectory, are in no way inferior to any of those we have mentioned. There are also the Benedictine monastery of St Lambrecht, fifty miles from Villach on the way to Udine, the Cistercian Abbey of Wilhering on the Danube, and finally yet another Benedictine building, that of Lambach, near Linz again, and in the centre of this most fertile district of monastic building.

The smaller towns of Austria deserve a few words, for they all contain notable works of the period we are studying. Salzburg, for instance, is one of the most beautiful of Baroque towns in existence. In addition to the buildings of Fischer von Erlach that have already been described there are numerous churches and convents. The Cathedral was built by an Italian, Solari, between 1614 and 1634, and has a high-altarpiece by Mascagni, an Italian artist of little merit whose works are often to be met with in Austria. The Benedictine Abbey of St Peter and the high-altar in the Franciscan church, that has been so skilfully arranged to contrast with the hexagonal choir and its tall, thin, Gothic columns, are excellent specimens of the style. The Residenz, where the Prince-Archbishop used to live, is uninteresting, but the stables, the summer riding-school, the winter riding-school with its ceiling painting of a tournament done in 1690, and the gallery connecting the Cathedral with the Residenz with its keystones of horses' heads, all these draw attention to the strange, equine predilection of one of the Archbishops. The Mirabell-Schloss, in the middle of the town, has a fine green copper roof and a staircase with early sculptures by Raphael Donner, where cupids appear to be sliding down the banisters ; and the garden has a long wall of apricot- and apple-trees, four great groups of sculptured rapes, a garden-theatre, and another little garden with stone dwarfs. Outside Salzburg, the château of Hellbrunn is famous for its gardens and for an elaborate water-organ in which hundreds of figures at different employments move to a strident and panting music ascribed to Mozart. The château, itself, is dull, and Mascagni's frescoes have added nothing to its qualities, but the water-organ, as a piece of misplaced industry, is an experience that will never be forgotten, so fertile are its possible developments of beauty.

Innsbruck has little in comparison. There are the Catholic casino, a specimen of the richest external stucco decoration that compares with the Falcon Inn of Würzburg; the church of St Jakob, and the Pfarrkirche, built by a good Tyrolese architect, Franz Penz, in 1751-1756, with fine stucco-work, and dome- and wall-paintings by M. Günther.

There is more to see in Gratz. This town seems curiously removed from both the German and Italian worlds; it is near Hungary and not far north of some of the most fervent Moslems in the whole of the world of Islam, yet nearly all its hundred and fifty thousand population are pure German in race. The churches of S. Andrea and of the Brothers of Mercy are specimens of late seventeenth-century Baroque, while the Cathedral was remodelled by an Italian, Pietro de Pomis (*d.* 1633), who left two votive pictures flanking the high-altar and designed the Mausoleum, a big Baroque affair next to the Cathedral, in which the Emperor Ferdinand II. lies buried. There are several smaller churches and the pilgrimage-shrine of Mariatrost outside the town. Laibach, a Slovene town between Gratz and Trieste, has two good Italian fountains and its Cathedral was frescoed by Quaglio, a pupil of Tiepolo. Linz, a town that we have had occasion to mention more than once because of the monasteries in its neighbourhood, has much good work : a Trinity column in the "guglia" fashion ; a marble statue of St John Nepomuk by Raphael Donner ; the Alte Domkirche, a Jesuit building of 1669-1682 ; and various smaller chapels and convents. Before leaving Austria attention should perhaps be drawn to the extraordinary pulpits at Traun-kirchen, Tautendorf, Fischlham, and Gaspoltshofen. These are modelled in the form of boats filled with statues of the disciples, which float upon a gilded and conventionalised water filled with dolphins or lobsters. In some cases the disciples are at the oars and sail is about to be hoisted. These pulpits are in small villages on the Austrian lakes.

Having dealt with practically every monument of importance in Austria we come now to Hungary. The distance between Vienna and Budapest is about a hundred and seventy miles, and the actual Hungarian frontier is only some thirty miles from the Austrian capital. Nearly every building of importance for our period is situated in that small part of Hungary lying between these two capitals. But Hungary, like Poland, is a *terra incognita* ; it is next to impossible to find even a photograph of any building. I have never yet, for example, seen an illustration of the châteaux of the Esterháza, though the fact that these extraordinary buildings have been taken away from Hungary and included in Yugo-Slavia might have encouraged this publication as a piece of national propaganda for its recovery. I wrote at some length on these two castles of Eisenstadt and Esterháza in *Southern Baroque Art* and will, there-fore, delay no longer over their details. Neither need Budapest be remarked upon at any length, because a fever of rebuilding has raged among its inhabitants for the last fifty years and has turned their city into one of the finest modern towns in Europe.

Pressburg, the first Hungarian town reached from Vienna,

was the seat of the Hungarian Diet and the crowning-place of the kings of Hungary. The members of the Diet met here, till 1848, in their national costume of fur cap, an attila or short frock-coat, a mantle or loose coat, usually lined with fur and used as a cloak, and tight pantaloons and boots; while the debates, till 1835, were carried on in Latin. The great Austrian sculptor, Raphael Donner, designed, in 1734, the Chapel of St Elemosinarius, and executed a leaden equestrian statue of St Martin dressed in Hungarian costume as a young Hussar. There was a fine eighteenth-century royal palace on a cliff above the river, but it was destroyed by fire during the Napoleonic wars.

We may take, as another typical Hungarian town, Gran—Esztergom in Hungarian—for its vast cathedral, though it was rebuilt in 1820, and does not therefore belong by date to our period, is Italianate in style, and finished with a magnificence that was rare after the eighteenth century. The reason for this exception is that Gran was the residence of the Primate of all Hungary, and that this prelate enjoyed an immense revenue from the great estates attached to the primacy. The Archduke Karl Ambrosius, the Primate who undertook most of this glorification, is buried in the cathedral in a tomb by Canova. The treasury contains an incredible collection of jewels, relics, and embroidered vestments.

It is difficult to find any more than this about Hungary. Even Kassa, where there is a Gothic cathedral built by the French Gothic architect Villard d'Honnecourt, remains undocumented; and Bartfa, Löcse, and the immense Benedictine abbey of Pannon-halma on a spur of the Bakony forest, the oldest and richest convent of Hungary, remain unknown to the outside world even in their mediæval remains. There must be much unstudied material in the small Hungarian towns, but at present there is no method of approach to the subject.

Prague, in contrast to Hungary, possesses a fully documented architectural history, and Prague has perhaps more buildings of the Baroque date than any town in Europe—a distinction it would, perhaps, have shared with Budapest had it not been for the Turks. Where we cannot bless that race of warriors we must thank the Jesuits, chief agent and instrument of church and convent building; it is due largely to their untiring zeal that Prague had great building activity during the seventeenth as well as the eighteenth centuries, so that its architecture has a continuity and development which are lacking in Vienna. During the first of these two centuries Milanese architects were employed, and it was Giovanni Marini, a native of Milan, who built the great Wallenstein's palace, between 1623 and 1630; there is a fine formal garden at the back with a bathing-pool, a riding-hall, and a grotto with stucco-work by another Milanese, Bartolommeo Bianco. The Royal Palace on the Hradcany contains Italian work of that same date, done for the Emperor Matthias by Vincenzo Scamozzi of Vicenza; finally, in the suburbs of the town there is the Belvedere, a villa of even earlier Italian date, for it was built for the Emperor Ferdinand I. by Paolo della Stella, a pupil of Jacobo Sansovino.

In the next century native architects began to take the place of Italians, and, in particular, the family of Dientzenhofer from Franconia came into eminence, culminating in Kilian Ignaz Dientzenhofer, 1690-1752, the contemporary and equal of Fischer von Erlach and Lukas von Hildebrandt. These buildings coming after an extremely good and vigorous provincial Gothic, far better than that of Nuremberg, make Prague into a supreme architectural delight; in some ways it is the most interesting town in Europe after Rome, Venice, and Naples.

Fischer von Erlach, as I mentioned a little way back, did

a certain amount of work in Prague, chiefly at the palace of Count Clam-Gallas, which he built between 1707 and 1712; while its magnificently carved doorway and the Hercules fountain in the courtyard are by a sculptor-architect, Matthias Braun, who was responsible for the great carved portal to the palace of Count Thun, and the monument in the cathedral to Field-Marshal Schlick. Fischer von Erlach also designed the monument to Chancellor Wratislaw von Mitrowitz in the Jakobskirche. There were a couple of good Italian architects, Anselmo and Carlo Luragho, who worked at this same date in Prague. The first helped Kilian Ignaz Dientzenhofer at the Kinsky Palace and worked a great deal in the Royal Palace, while the second designed the monastery of the Bohemian Order of the Cross, the Kreuzherrenstift, and the porch to the Salvator church.

Kilian Ignaz Dientzenhofer besides building the Kinsky Palace gave designs for the Palace of Count Nostitz. But far more important than these are the Jesuit Church of St Nicholas, begun by Christopher Dientzenhofer and finished by him; the Church of St John Nepomuk of the Rock, which is approached by two great flights of stairs; and his remodelling of the octagonal Gothic Karlof church built by Peter Parler in the fourteenth century. A good example of German smaller domestic building is the Amerika Casino, or Zwergenhaus, in the Karlshofergasse, Neustadt, a square suburban villa of an ideal perfection, with its windows and doorways most admirably spaced. A similar and even better instance is the Concordia at Bamberg by Johann Dientzenhofer, which will be described later on when Franconia, the native home of the Dientzenhofer family, is reached.

But there are numerous other Baroque buildings in Prague not yet mentioned. The Old-Town Bridge Tower with its twenty-eight statues and groups of saints, the majority of them early eighteenth-century work ; the Clementinum, a huge enclosure of churches, chapels, colleges, and convents, built by the Jesuits, almost, in fact, a Jesuit Kremlin ; the church and most of the conventual buildings of the Premonstratensian Abbey of Strahof ; the Church of Loretto with its incredible treasury ; and the palace of the Prince-Archbishop and the Priory of the Knights of Malta.

Many lesser towns in Bohemia contain important monuments of the period : Brünn, Olmütz, and Znaim for example, all three of which have Trinity columns, or some other variety of the Southern Italian " guglia," rich Jesuit convents and churches, and the palaces of their prelates—these dignitaries, in the case of the two former towns, having the rank of Prince-Bishop. In Bohemia, as in Hungary, there are, finally, the châteaux of the nobles, whose estates reach to unprecedented dimensions and confer plutocratic opportunities upon their possessors. There is the château of Count Waldstein at Dux, near to the famous Cistercian Abbey of Osseg, and in this castle the old Casanova read through his love-letters and composed his memoirs while he worked as librarian for the Count ; Schloss Krummau, a castle of Prince Schwarzenberg, with its drawbridge, tilting-yard and its barrack for the Prince's lifeguard of forty grenadiers ; and Wilfersdorf, a castle of Prince Liechtenstein, whence his estates—and the independent principality of Liechtenstein is not included in this—stretch away for two hundred miles to the frontier of Silesia.

Austrian Poland and Galicia remain, like Hungary, an unexplored land. But Cracow contains good baroque and rococo buildings ; there are a few great Catholic monasteries, mostly rebuilt in the seventeenth century, and there are towns like Tarnow where the cathedral is said to contain very curious monuments to the Ostrog and Tarnowski families ; they are of marble, richly adorned with statues and bas-reliefs of battles, most interesting in their rendering of Polish and Galician costumes, and they reach up to the roof of the church, a height of sixty or seventy feet. Farther south than this, at Suczawitzka, in the Bukowina, there are curious embroidered tomb-covers to the princes of the Mogila family, and these in their costume and their ornament are the beginning, the most westerly, points of a quite unstudied development of the baroque that had its centre in the Ukraine and made a union from the two bastards of Italian and Byzantine art. Many churches and monasteries in this style were built at Kief and in its neighbourhood, and their influence reached as far as Northern Persia, where some of the mosques, the town walls, or the town gates with their gaudy tile-pictures, are of a definitely Baroque character, but of that far-away and provincial expression to be found in Portugal, in Mexico, or in Brazil.

We have now dealt, in a bare outline, with the three chief provinces of the ancient Austrian Empire, and there remain to be discussed the former states of the Holy Roman Empire, the modern Germany, in fact. These we shall consider in the following order :—Bavaria, Saxony, Prussia, and finally the smaller states and the ecclesiastical principalities.

Bavarian architecture possesses its distinct character, so that it is as easy to distinguish a Bavarian building as it is to pick out from a heap of photographs what is typically Bohemian from what is obviously Viennese. Even so, there are certain distinctions to be drawn ; for there are now included in Bavaria districts like Franconia, the architecture in which is of an emphatically more northern variety than that to be found in Munich or Augsburg. As Würzburg, Bamberg, and Bayreuth, the three chief towns of Franconia, were formerly independent, both of each other and of

Bavaria, we shall in this case subtract them once more from that latter country and consider them later on in the book in the space devoted to the lesser principalities and bishoprics.

We will begin, then, with Munich, in which town the large and untidily planned Royal Palace contains, with a good deal of earlier work, and yet more of the distinctively early nineteenth-century Munich style, a set of state-rooms furnished with full Royal rig-out of our period. The gilt is almost too gold; the curtains breathless; the ceiling heavy and frowning: yet some details have great beauty, and in the stucco decorations there are signs of a lightness of touch that one comes gradually to associate with the Frenchman, François Cuvilliés. There is, in particular, a long narrow saloon built so as to show off a great collection of china figures, where there is some splendid furniture made by Miroffsky to the designs of Cuvilliés, which was not visible to the general public till the overthrow of the Wittelsbachs at the end of the war, the sight of which forms a good prelude to the view of his two chief works in this neighbourhood. The more easily accessible of these is the Residenz-Theater, just behind the palace, which he designed and built between 1752 and 1760—the most perfect setting imaginable for a Mozart opera, for the whole affair looks as though it would fade away and dissolve with the end of each air. This is rococo art at its absolute culmination, and anyone who wishes for a definition of what difference there is between those two misleading terms —Baroque and Rococo—can do no better than visit and compare in his mind this Residenz-Theater in Munich and the opera-house built at almost precisely the same date by a member of the Bibbiena family at Bayreuth.[1]

[1] Other works of Cuvilliés are the Piosasque de Non palace in the Theater-strasse at Munich, the façade of the Archbishop's Palace, and the Schloss Hainhausen.

Outside the city, in the park of Nymphenburg, the other Cuvilliés masterpiece can be seen. The palace itself is a little uninteresting, compared at any rate with one's first anticipation of it as it comes into view in the centre of its huge semi-cycle of low white buildings, in one wing of which the old Nymphenburg porcelain, most beautiful of German wares, used to be made. The other side the great garden stretches away, and on both sides there are long stretches of canal, for the Electors used to come here by barge from their capital. Early autumn is the time to visit this garden, when there is a little mist above the water and the ground has its first fall of leaves. Each new corner through the woods brings some fresh lake into view, and there is usually a pavilion of some kind, the Badenburg or the Pagodenburg, near to the water's edge. The trees and water, though the two are difficult to tell apart, so clearly do the gold boughs answer out of this willing echo, key up the senses to the expectancy of some mortal counterpart of all this natural beauty. A little pavilion called the Amalienburg is the climax. This is the second masterpiece of Cuvilliés, and is one of the three or four supreme proofs of rococo art. It is a low, one-storeyed, white building with a little graceful stucco-work above the windows, and in its smallness it contains but two rooms, a bedroom and a saloon, beside the lobbies and the Dutch-tiled kitchen. The bedroom has decorations in the most lavish and superb gold work that has ever been seen, but of a gold that is strongly impregnated with orange-yellow. The back of the alcove where the bed stood shows a kind of crackling fire of design, which is answered by every mirror and picture-frame round the room. Above the mantelpiece there is a portrait of the Elector Max III. Joseph, with gun and dog ready to set off hunting. All this is, however, but the foil to the larger room that lies beyond, and it is a wonderful moment when the door is opened and that extra-ordinary silver network is seen, glistening and gleaming from the walls. The room, which is in reality circular, with a domed roof, has had its walls converted into an octagon by Cuvilliés, and each wall has a great central mirror made of square pool-like panels. Above these mirrors and round the cornice there is an unimaginable richness and delicacy combined, for the silver stucco-work in its elaboration has taken on the most varied and far-fetched motives, musical instruments, weapons of war, trophies of the chase, huge silver birds and fishes, nets like shimmering scales, diapered work, drums and flags, and sprays of flowers all combining under this magical touch, which is like the hand of hoar-frost on tree and flower, and is yet not so much cold as cool, a refreshment for hot weather. It has something indescribably temporary in its appearance, as though the whole of this scene had been easily and quickly made out of the two coolest things known to the senses — a field of snow and a waterfall. It possesses the ease and swiftness of some diverti-mento or serenade by Mozart, and it may well end as gently, fading away from the eyes before one can understand how it ever stood there to be inhabited. There is nothing else that quite equals this pavilion ; for it is the supreme monument to its period, as are, to their respective ages, the Alhambra and the Capella Palatina.

Schleissheim, a few miles from Munich in another direction, has another Schloss of the late seventeenth century, built for the Elector Max Emmanuel by Josef Effner, the architect of the Preysing Palace in Munich ; but this is of the large, thoroughly Baroque type, with a typical German staircase and great hall above, on the first floor. There are the remains of an extremely beautiful garden, with a long canal stretching away down to the

Lustheim, a smaller Schloss at the far end ; for this is again, like Nymphenburg, a domain within which they travelled by barge. Both Schleissheim and Nymphenburg have great painted views of other Bavarian Royal châteaux hung in passages where they are but dimly seen, and a study of these would show many most beautiful and elaborate parterres with ingenious devices for the use and exploitation of water.

The actual town of Munich has many buildings of our period, not yet enumerated, which are of interest. There is the Johann-Nepomuk church, built between 1733 and 1746 by the brothers Cosmas Damian and Egid Quirin Asam, two most remarkable men. The very tall portal has those typical down-flowing and outspreading lines, typical of the date, which in this particular case form themselves into a complicated rockery of stucco each side of the door. At either flank of the church there are houses, formerly convents, of delightful and elaborate richness of decoration, and of course the church interior is decorated with the usual lavish and loaded richness. Another church, the Theatine, built by the Italian architect Barelli between 1662 and 1675, has an interior of an elaboration that one is more wont to associate with Naples than with Munich. There are, in conclusion, one or two private houses of charming design, notably the Preysing Palace, which has a staircase of Viennese elegance.

Augsburg, one of the most delightful towns of Central Europe, has its mediæval excellence continued architecturally into the eighteenth century. The Barfüsser Kirche and the Golden Hall of the Rathaus deserve more than a mere mention, while the best hotel in the town, the " Drei Mohren," has a fine six-columned façade, with four floors of elaborately festooned windows, and three storeys of dormer windows above that. It was built, almost exactly two hundred years ago, by the Munich architect, Johann Gunetsrhainer.

Saxony is our next subject, and the Electors of this extremely rich province of Germany seem to have shown extravagance in two directions : their collection of gems and their picture gallery. In the way of building they would not seem to have accomplished any very remarkable achievements. The palace is a duller, a more complicated, and a more restored version of the Royal Palace at Munich, while the Grüne Gewölbe, the vaults in which the collection of gems are housed, remind one of the Medici treasure in Florence. Just opposite the palace is the Catholic Court Church, like an immense enlargement of St Mary-le-Strand in London ; it is of Italianate design, like that fine church of Gibbs', and was built by the architect Gaetano Chiaveri between 1738 and 1751. It contains, naturally enough, an altarpiece by the Saxon painter, Raphael Mengs. There is another interesting church at Dresden, the Frauen Kirche, a Protestant building of 1726-1738, by the architect George Bähr, with a heavy stone dome and an interior disposed in decks like the section of a liner. Across the Elbe, in the Neustadt, there are two objects of interest, a gilded copper equestrian statue of Augustus the Strong by Wiedemann of Augsburg, and the so-called Japanese Palace built by Count Flemming in 1715, and purchased later by the same Elector Augustus II. This latter has the remains of a fine formal garden stretching down to the river-bank. Opposite, across the water, is the Brühl Terrace, which that profligate minister of Augustus III. built as a kind of promenade for his palace, since burnt down. The best documentation for our period is the set of paintings of Dresden and its environs by Bernardo Bellotto, which are now in the Dresden picture gallery, and in which the artist renders the strange, opaque, milky colour of Saxony with extraordinary clearness. Some pictures of Warsaw belonging to the same series have a peculiar fascination, from the Polish costumes worn by the figures, and also because Poland remains the most unstudied of European countries with regard to its art and architecture.

We must now account for what we have purposely left till last in our description of Dresden—the Zwinger. This is one of the strangest products of the Late Renaissance, quite unlike anything else in history till the Paris Exhibition of 1900. It was built between 1711 and 1722 by Poeppelmann, the architect of Augustus II. It consists of a great court surrounded by a gallery and by seven pavilions, and is the mere fragment, just the courtyard in fact, to a palace and a garden that were meant to stretch down to the banks of the Elbe that flows some two or three hundred yards away. There is much fantastic sculpture, some of it by Balthasar Permoser, in this same exhibition taste, and the whole affair is a kind of prelude to the Art Nouveau with which this present century began under the auspices of such men as Monsieur Bing, the enthusiast for everything twisted or noisy in Japanese art. There are pictures by Bellotto in the gallery at Dresden that show the courtyard full of great coaches and alive with a gaily dressed crowd, while the present picture gallery, that occupies the whole of one side of the Zwinger, disgorges tired visitors into this strange court in precisely the sort of mood in which they are most likely to appreciate the gaiety and coolness of such exhibition architecture. After the great pictures of the collection have grown familiar it is pleasant to visit the room full of views of Dresden by Bellotto, who rendered the milky-white opaque light of this city, the northern wintry architecture, and the half-German and half-Polish crowd with more skill and more arrangement than is possible with a film.

Prussia next ; and there is not much to it, save Potsdam, for Berlin is essentially a city of the " thirties and forties," while anything that survived that period of an apeing of St Petersburg classicism was improved out of all taste by the late, too scrupulous, Kaiser.

The palace, most hideous of its race, was built by that indifferent architect, Schlüter—chiefly between 1698 and 1716. The façades are very ugly, the interior court tolerable ; while the two great saloons with stucco decorations by this same hand show the eighteenth century in nefarious competition with our own for the prize of clumsy ugliness. Schlüter's equestrian statue of the Great Elector, just outside the palace, is a better sample of his powers, but even this is commonplace and too solid. The Schloss at Charlottenburg, a suburb of Berlin, is also by Schlüter, but it was remodelled later by Eosander von Goethe and by Knöbelsdorff, and it contains the most beautiful and delicate rococo decorations that give a hint of the extraordinary loveliness of the work at Potsdam.

This latter place is beyond any doubt one of the great achievements of Europe and as fine in its way as anything to be seen. It is the eighteenth century at the absolute summit of its achievement. The town is full of delightful buildings, but interest centres round three palaces—the Town Palace, the New Palace, and Sanssouci. The first of these—all three of them are the work of Frederick the Great—has beautiful colonnades projecting from the façades in the kind of taste that one associates with a good theatrical drawing of that time, and has never seen elsewhere in actual stone. Inside the palace are some of those rooms with silvered boiseries that, once Potsdam has been visited, are associated for evermore with this pleasant oasis in the Prussian sands. The New Palace, which according to tradition was built by Frederick out of ostentation in the middle of the Seven Years' War, is the best of the three. It was designed by S. G. Büring, an architect from Hamburg. Opposite the florid red brick, somewhat Dutch, house there are appropriate stables of fine fantastic conception, planned to balance the great mass of the palace. Inside there are two floors, in which the French art of the period at its highest expression can be seen to absolute perfection. The boiseried rooms decorated in silver are quite inconceivable in their loveliness ; many of the doors have a wave-like, waterfall treatment which is again echoed in some of the wall-panels in two shades of gold, or with a greenish silver that gives variety to that more conventional shade of moonlight. The rooms are full of superb furniture of the date, and pictures by Watteau can surely have never found a more congenial environment. Sanssouci is much smaller, merely a one-storeyed flight of pavilions, but the rooms are, again, the very finest example of their kind. It was designed by G. W. von Knöbelsdorff. For some reason Sanssouci is always mentioned as the most beautiful of the Potsdam palaces, whereas the New Palace has better work ; probably this is because, until these days of the German Republic, it was impossible to get admittance to this latter, while Sanssouci was always open to the public. In any case, French art can be seen here as it cannot be seen in France, and as it can be seen nowhere else save in the gardens of San Ildefonso in Spain, and at Peterhof in Russia. There is enough beauty here to reconcile the conscience that can be so often outraged at the sight of Louis XV. furniture and all the abomination of skill that one connects with Gouthière or Caffieri.

There is not much else of our period in the modern Prussia. Brunswick and Hanover have palaces that were remodelled early in the last century, and Herrenhausen, the summer palace of the Guelphs, a few miles out of the latter town, is not of interest save to those who are engrossed in the study of the first Hanoverian Kings of England.

We will now deal with Silesia, and must first of all draw attention to Heinrichau, where there is an immense Cistercian convent, a good church, and, in front of it all, a regular " guglia " in that particular Southern brand of taste, almost churriguerresque in feeling, that we learn to associate with Silesia. Breslau, the capital of this province, has innumerable fine old houses and the University, a former Jesuit college, of huge size and excellent design with magnificent rooms in the interior, but the name of the architect is uncertain. Breslau has a character of its own, half-Bohemian, perhaps, and half-Polish, and its buildings serve to draw our interest towards that latter country, the most un-studied of European lands. In the same province there is the beautiful Cistercian convent of Grüssau, an immense Baroque building equal in scale to the Cistercian convent of Oliva, near Dantzig.

We next transfer our investigations to Cassel, the former capital of the Electors of Hesse. The princes of this house had great wealth, derived in part from that incredible system of hiring out their own subjects as soldiers to foreign Powers—can obedience be carried further than this ? With the proceeds of such traffic they built Wilhelmshöhe, their summer palace, outside the town. An Italian, Giov. Franc. Guernieri, was responsible for the general design, more particularly for the garden lay-out. The cascades are fearful and wonderful, but the general level of taste is perhaps signified by the fact that the point of the whole garden, the source and principle of the cascade, is a copy, thirty feet high, of the Farnese Hercules, while the Moorish and Chinese pavilions, dotted about, show the decline of the garden tradition and recall Schwetzingen, that ugly garden of the Electors Palatine, near Heidelberg. The earlier work must have been overlaid and improved towards the end of the century when the taste for English gardens had come into fashion.

Our way leads south again, in order to deal with Franconia, the Electorates, and the Rhine cities. Franconia we may conceive of as having three centres : Würzburg, Bamberg, and Bayreuth. The first of these was the chief working ground of J. B. Neumann, the fourth great architect of Germany, and the equal of Fischer von Erlach, Lukas von Hildebrandt, and Kilian Ignaz Dientzenhofer. He built the Schloss at Würzburg between 1720 and 1744, his plans being sent from time to time to de Cotte, or to some other French architect for correction and advice. This supervision must have hampered Neumann more than it helped him, but on the other hand the construction of this finest of all German palaces must have been aided in no little degree by the fact that it is late in date and that all the fine buildings of Vienna were finished almost before Würzburg was begun. The palace is of truly prodigious size and is built in a yellow, almost golden, stone that carries carving admirably ; its erection was due to the Prince-Bishop Johann Philip, a member of the Schönborn family, by whom the castle of Pommersfelden was built. The Schönborns covered Franconia with buildings, and I believe I am right in saying that it was three brothers, who were respectively the eldest son and head of the family, the Prince-Bishop of Würzburg, and the Bishop of Bamberg, to whom so many palaces are due.

The staircase, as I have said before, is, with those of the Belvedere, Brühl, and Pommersfelden, one of the four finest in all Germany. It is magnificent from its size : perhaps severe

E

criticism might not place this as the most inspired of Neumann's projects. This staircase, indeed, might almost lead in an idealised world from the various platforms up to a railway restaurant above, but Tiepolo has contrived to roof it with the sort of Nirvana to which no railway ever led. He worked on it for the two years 1752 and 1753, painting Olympus in the middle and the four quarters of the globe in the corners. It is a supreme example of Italian decorative painting, overflowing with life and yet not crowded, while, merely as a piece of sustained imagination, it exceeds the other great achievements of this school. Of this kind of painting I should cite the following as masterpieces of their kind : the rooms by Pietro da Cortona in the Barberini and Ros-pigliosi palaces in Rome, the great staircase of the Escurial and the saloon in the Palazzo Riccardi at Florence by Luca Giordano ; and Tiepolo's own achievements at the Palazzo Labia in Venice and the Palazzo Clerici in Milan. Out of all these six only Luca Giordano's staircase at the Escurial can be really compared with Tiepolo on this immense roof in Würzburg ; but in the few years that he worked at this palace he painted, also, the Kaisersaal, a room where the Holy Roman Emperors held receptions when on their way from Vienna to Frankfurt to be crowned. Here, his decoration instead of being let loose on to a huge surface has been confined into compartments, where he has represented the marriage of Frederick Barbarossa with Beatrix of Burgundy, which had taken place at Würzburg in a past that must have seemed even more remote from his day than it does from ours. The white and pink marble of the room ; the great chimney-pieces with the huge portraits of Prince-Bishops above them ; and the terraced gardens, as in an old formal theatre-scene, that rise up outside the windows make this Kaisersaal into one of the most romantic halls imaginable, with the Venetian histrion at work above, who puts his fellow-actors into such silks and brocades as the painters of his race have always loved.

Most of the rooms in the Schloss have been modernised and ruined in the Empire style, but there is still a nice hall downstairs at the foot of the staircase decorated in Christmas-cracker style with little bits of mirror and fresco-paintings by Zick, an artist we shall come across later on. Upstairs, among the rooms leading from the Kaisersaal, is a most beautiful mirror-room in green lacquer with a stuccoed and gilded ceiling, from which we give an illustration, of surpassing poetry and imagination. The tapestry-room has three pieces of Italian comedians woven by C. Perot and designed by a Swiss painter, Rudolf Byss (*b*. Soleure, 1660; *d*. Würzburg, 1735). There are said to be two more pieces in the store of the Schloss, so that originally the hanging must have consisted of five tapestries; and it is sufficient to say that these tapestries, with the book mentioned some way back by Gregorio Lambranzi, are among the supreme things in the whole history of theatrical art. There are, as I have said, beautiful terraced gardens behind the palace; there is also an orangery, and the gardens are entered from the town by several iron gates of superb design by Johann Georg and Anton Oegg, taller and more elaborate than Tijou's gates at Hampton Court. The palace chapel, also by Neumann, has two altarpieces by Tiepolo, and it is one of the best smaller church interiors of this date in Germany, comparing favourably with the Johann-Nepomuk church in Munich.

There are other good buildings in Würzburg; at one corner of the cathedral is the Schönborn mortuary chapel, also by Neumann; and near by, in the town, is the Falcon Inn, a most peculiar example of rich external stucco decoration, on its way to the methods of the aforementioned Monsieur Bing, and

very much like the Casino of the Catholic Club in Innsbruck.
A few miles outside the town is the Prince-Bishop's garden of
Veitshöchheim, which the guide-books stupidly say is meant as
a copy of Versailles. As a matter of fact it is nothing of the
kind ; it happens to be of extremely original design, and is one
of the most romantically beautiful gardens in Europe, absolutely
untouched by the landscapists of a later generation, and complete
with a whole population of statues and shell-work divinities. I
have been unable to discover the name of the architect of this
garden, but I suspect Italian interference, which, as ever, was for
the good.

Bamberg seems like the authentic centre of Germany.
During the Middle Ages it was the focus of witch-burning, and
much of that acrid smoke seems still to hang about these dark
spires and mysterious quiet streets. The Residenz, or palace
of the Bishops, was built by one of the Schönborn family. Its
chief interest is a room painted by Fra Pozzo with extraordinary
imaginary portraits of the House of Hapsburg, and a continual
fight against the Turks in progress—very good scene-painting.
There is a wonderful old house in the Judengasse heavily hung
with masks and grotesques, and a little farther down the street is
the Concordia, an ancient Club or Guild house of extraordinary
beauty. It is on the banks of the river, and the house and small
garden are attributed to the architect Johann Dientzenhofer.
The Town Hall is on an island in the river, and has two gates,
above which there are balconies of much elaboration by the
sculptor J. B. Mutschelle. Twelve miles away is Pommersfelden,
the finest private house in Germany, and the seat of the Schönborn
family. It was the two brothers of Count Schönborn, Johann
Philip Franz and Friedrich Karl, who built the palaces at
Würzburg, Bamberg, and Bruchsal. There is also a fine

Schönborn castle designed by Lukas von Hildebrandt near Göllersdorff in Bohemia. Pommersfelden was designed and built by the brothers Leonhard and Johann Dientzenhofer, and its finest feature is the staircase, of which we give an illustration. The elaborately painted ceiling is by J. R. Byss, the designer of the theatrical tapestries at Würzburg.

The immense Cistercian monastery of Ebrach is also near Bamberg. It was remodelled by an Italian, Bossi ; its conventual buildings were rebuilt by Leonhard Dientzenhofer ; and it was finally enlarged by J. B. Neumann. It possesses the most magnificent wrought-iron gates in existence, also a staircase not far inferior to that at Pommersfelden. Both of these are illustrated in this book. When dissolved during the Napoleonic wars it owned 25,000 acres of forest, the best vineyards in Franconia, fifty-four villages, and an income of 200,000 florins. The sale of its estates brought in 750,000 florins : it was as wealthy as Melk or Göttweig.

Bayreuth is an example of the small town in perfection ; and those who admire the architecture of the little Cotswold towns would be forced to admit that Burford, Chipping Camden, and Broadway are but minor specimens of this ideal of excellence. There is here a bucolic atmosphere of peculiar beauty and in-spiration, starting off nobly with the equestrian statue of the Margrave Christian Ernest that stands in front of the palace. He was a field-marshal in the Emperor's service, but even this position can hardly be held to justify the allegories of the four quarters of the globe that surround him, and the dwarf that holds the bridle of his horse. In spite of this exaggeration, the town over which he ruled has great claims to eminence, besides the Wagner Theatre. There is, in the first place, the old opera-house built by the great Giuseppe Bibbiena in 1750, the most beautiful of its kind in existence, and perhaps the only perfect piece of work left us by that great dynasty of theatrical architects. The palace has fine rooms and a good formal garden, while two churches contain typically humorous stucco works of the period. On a hill-side above the town, and not very far from the Wagner Theatre, is the suburb of St Georgen, which was built by the Margrave George William early in the eighteenth century. The church and the chapter-house of an Order founded by this Margrave, and changed by his successor, George Frederick Charles, to the Order of the Red Eagle, are interesting because of the minutiæ of this miniature kingdom. However, the great beauty of Bayreuth is the Eremitage, a summer palace built by George William in 1715. It was designed by St Pierre, a French architect, and the palace, together with the Temple of the Sun and its two detached semicircular colonnades, have rooms in the most far-fetched Rococo taste, particularly a kind of summer arbour where there are orange-trees growing in stucco relief out of the walls. A detailed description of this garden can be found in my brother's book—*Discursions*.

We are left now to a consideration of the minor principalities and bishoprics of Germany, and there are a few not yet dealt with in the North before we reach the Rhine provinces : Dessau, for instance, not far from Magdeburg and the capital of the Duchy of Anhalt. The chief interest here is in the palace and gardens of Wörlitz, twelve miles away. There are a number of temples and pavilions scattered about the grounds among which a great collection of pictures, chiefly inherited from a Princess of Orange, are distributed, including all the works of a local painter named Abraham Snaphau (1641-1691), who can be studied nowhere else. Gotha and Weimar are more interesting for their literary or musical associations than as possessing any distinctive building of our period. Every capital of a duchy or principality is sure to contain some interesting work, and therefore while there is not space to give details, it may be taken for certain that Oldenburg, Schwerin, or Zerbst is worth investigation.

The Rhine provinces possess a whole plethora of buildings; but the finest thing of our period in this whole region is the palace of Brühl, near Cologne and on the way to Bonn. This was built between 1725 and 1728 by the Elector Clement Augustus, a Bavarian prince and brother to the Emperor Charles VII. (1697-1745) who was proclaimed Holy Roman Emperor on the death of Charles VI., the last male Hapsburg, but had soon to surrender his pretensions to Maria Theresa and her husband, Charles of Lorraine. The palace was designed by Johann Conrad Schlaun, but many French artists worked upon its details. The staircase, of which we give an illustration, was constructed between 1740 and 1748 under the influence, if not the direction, of J. B. Neumann; the great trophy upon the wall was made by a Frenchman, Brillie, as late as 1766; the frescoed ceiling, on the other hand, is by Nicholas Stüber, and bears the date 1732. In fact, this masterpiece of its period must have been, from first to last, about forty years under construction. The rooms of the Elector are decorated by Michel Leveilly after the plans of François Cuvilliés, and the Salle des Gardes has a painted ceiling that shows the apotheosis of Charles VII., a most entertaining and amusing affair.

Not very far from Brühl, the Elector had another château, called Pöppelsdorf. This was built by Robert de Cotte between 1715 and 1740, and is of quadrangular plan enclosing a circular arcaded court. Cologne, on the other hand, has little, or nothing, to offer us, and we do not come across any other thing of importance till Bonn is reached. Here there is an immense palace of the Electors of Cologne, who always, and wisely, chose Bonn for their residence in preference to that city. This palace is to the designs of Robert de Cotte, and an Italian, Enrico Zuccali. There is also a delightful Town Hall by the Frenchman, Michel Leveilly, while on a hill called the Kreuzberg, behind Pöppelsdorf, there stands a Servite convent with a marble imitation of the Scala Santa at Rome which was built by the Elector Clement Augustus. Underneath is a vault with some two dozen mummified monks in glass cases. Neuwied, near by, the capital of a little mediatised principality, is a small model town of the period with a summer palace and gardens called Monrepos.

Coblentz is now at hand. Here there is a palace built by the last Elector of Treves, Clement Wenceslaus, Prince of Poland and Saxony and uncle to Louis XVI. The next of the Rhine Electorates is that of Maintz, where the Elector was Archbishop, premier Prince of Germany, and presided over the Imperial Diet ; their palace, like that of Coblentz, contains nothing of interest, but their Baroque tombs are to be seen in the cathedral. In life, these sculptured absurdities were of great importance. Their dominions were 150 German square miles, with a population of 400,000, and a revenue of 1½ million florins. They maintained a bodyguard of 2000 men, and a squadron of hussars.

The town of Treves, for we here make an excursion down the Moselle, is the most interesting of these towns. It has the Elector's Palace, a fine affair with a superb staircase by Johann Seiz, rather in the manner of Würzburg, and in support of this suggestion there is work by J. B. Neumann in the Church of St Paulin. Darmstadt, the capital of Hesse Darmstadt, and

72

Carlsruhe, the capital of Baden, do not contain any buildings of much importance in our period. We now come to the dominions of the Elector Palatine, though we must delay for a second in order to draw attention to Bruchsal, where there is a palace of the Prince-Bishop of Trier, built from the designs of J. B. Neumann to the order of that member of the Schönborn family who built Würzburg. There is here one of the best specimens of the German ceremonial staircase; and most fantastic apotheoses in fresco by a father and son, Johann and Januarius Zick. The latter, 1733-1797, was a pupil of Raphael Mengs in Rome, and was Court painter at Coblentz. Hyperbole can never have been carried farther, even in the East, than it is at Bruchsal. There are, also, many beautiful rooms with amusing ecclesiastical portraits, and the remnants of a garden through which the railway runs; in fact the stone statues of Swiss Guards are seen from the train. The Peterskirche at Bruchsal, with the episcopal vault, are also by J. B. Neumann. The Electors Palatine, of whom we gave the alarm a few lines back, deserted their true capital, Heidelberg, in 1720, and moved to Mannheim, where they built a palace of immeasurable size, and appropriate ugliness and lack of interest, to the designs of Joh. Clem. Froiment, an architect lent to the Elector Karl Philip by the Prince-Bishop of Speier. However, Mannheim has its compensations in the shape of the Church of St Ignatius, a most excellent affair of its type and due to the great Alessandro Galli Bibbiena (1687-1769), who also contrived the Town Hall, in front of which there is a complicated monument called the "Pyramide," by his compatriot Gabriele de Grupello (1644-1730). Not far from Mannheim there is another specimen of Bibbiena's work in the gardens and orangeries of the Elector's garden at Schwetzingen. Unfortunately the gardens were entirely ruined late in the eighteenth

century, but the hemicycles that form the orangeries still remain, with their colonnades unspoilt.

Near to this place is Stuttgart, the capital of Wurtemberg, where we must note the palace from designs by a Frenchman, P. L. de la Guêpière. But the real interest of this kingdom is the town of Ludwigsburg, laid out on a regular plan by Duke Eberhard Ludwig, with a palace by the Frenchman, J. F. Nette, and the Italian, Donato Giuseppe Frizoni; while there are two smaller palaces called Favorite and Monrepos, all three of these being in the midst of gardens. Ludwigsburg is one of the most interesting places of our period in Germany.

If there are any more places deserving mention, Fulda, the former seat of a Prince-Bishop, has perhaps the greatest claims. There is the Cathedral by Johann Dientzenhofer of Bamberg, and the Seminary by the same hand; also the Orangery, a summer palace of the Prince-Bishop, by Maximilian von Welsch, with a great sculptured flower-vase of rare beauty in front of it, more in the form of a Neapolitan " guglia." Fulda deserves a careful visit.

We have now come to the end of our itinerary, and I have saved till last a group of great abbeys in Southern Germany, some of them in Bavaria and some in Wurtemberg. But they must be dealt with together and so I have collected them into a few paragraphs at the last. Perhaps Kloster Ebrach, near Bamberg, should have been reserved till this point, but it is a long way north of these other abbeys. We come, now, to the fifth of the great German architects of the eighteenth century, Johann Michael Fischer, 1691-1766; he is more a decorator than a constructor; his façades are undistinguished, but he devised the most sumptuous church-interiors, carrying these abbeys into a degree of fantasy that cannot be matched anywhere else save in the Spanish-Indian buildings of Mexico.

The finest of all these monasteries is the Benedictine Abbey of Ottobeuren, about thirty miles south of Ulm. This was built by J. M. Fischer between 1737 and 1766. It is the most important Rococo building of Southern Germany. The church has two towers, and a great dome over the crossing. In the interior, the cupola is elaborately frescoed, and the large high-altar, the choir-stalls with their gilded reliefs, and the organs are all of surpassing excellence. We give an illustration of one of the wrought-iron gates of the choir. The outer sacristy has wonderful renaissance vestment-cupboards, and the conventual buildings have fine cloisters, a Kaisersaal with sixteen gilded statues of Hapsburg Emperors, and a superb library.

In this same district, near Ulm, is the monastery of Zwiefalten, now a lunatic asylum, so that only the church is accessible. This was of a splendour equal to that of Ottobeuren ; and Zwiefalten, like Ottobeuren, is the work of J. M. Fischer, who also built Fürstenzell, and a convent at Rott am Inn. There is also the Benedictine Abbey of Wiblingen, near Ulm, now a barracks. This has a splendidly decorated library, and the church is typically painted by Januarius Zick.

The Benedictine *Abbey of* Weingarten, near Ravensburg, was designed between 1715 and 1722 by an architect named Franz Beer, and it is the finest Rococo building of the Vorarlberg district. It was, also, worked upon by Christian Thumb, Andreas Schreck, and Donato Giuseppe Frizoni ; the ceiling frescoes, in church and library, are by C. D. Asam, one of the two architect brothers of Munich whom we have had occasion to mention before. He also painted the Maria-Viktoriasaal at Ingoldstadt. The choir-stalls are admirably elaborate, and the stucco-work is by a master called Schmuzer. Many of the Guelph family are buried in this monastery. The same stucco worker, Schmuzer, did a lot of decorations at Obermarschtal, an old Premonstratensian Abbey, now a château of Prince Thurn and Taxis.   Other fine churches are at Wolfegg and Kissleg on the Zeller-See, and at Ochsenhausen, near Biberach, where there is a Benedictine Abbey, now turned into a school and orphanage.   Near to this latter is the Premonstratensian Abbey, now a lunatic asylum, of Schussen-ried ; this, besides its church, has a particularly magnificent library-hall, decorated in 1754 with paintings by F. Hermann. Fifteen miles from Munich is the Cistercian Abbey of Fürstenfeld, now a barracks, with a good church of 1673-1732.   Then there is Osterhofen, near the Lake of Schliersee, with fine altars by Egid Quirin Asam, and the Benedictine Abbey of Weltenburg, on the early reaches of the Danube, between Ratisbon and Donauwörth ; this is another of the foundations of Duke Tassilo of Bavaria, like the Abbey of Kremsmünster; it was rebuilt in the eighteenth century by Cosmas Damian and Egid Quirin Asam, and has a very fine church.   Metten, an old Benedictine Abbey of which Charle-magne was the founder, between Deggendorf and Eisenstein in the Bavarian forest, is another typical monastery of this class with good rococo church and a library with unusual caryatid groups supporting its roof.   Even the smaller convents have great interest : as an example we may quote the Abbey of Diessen on the Lake of Ammersee, between Munich and the frontier of the Tyrol, the church of which contains altarpieces by G. B. Tiepolo and by G. B. Piazzetta.   At Waldsassen, between Leipzig and Munich, there is a magnificent Cistercian Abbey of Baroque date full of first-rate work, and there are more things of the same kind in the old Abbey of Amorbach, between Frankfort and Nuremberg.

On the way from Bamberg to Munich there are the two great Benedictine Abbeys of Banz and Vierzehnheiligen.   The former is a great building designed by both J. B. Neumann and

76

Johann Dientzenhofer.[1]   The latter monastery, of smaller size, because it is only a pilgrimage - shrine, is entirely by J. B. Neumann.   The interior is of an indescribable magnificence, though perhaps J. M. Fischer was the most successful purveyor of these effects.

In order to complete this group of abbeys we will include the Benedictine Abbey of Einsiedeln in Switzerland.   It was built by two brothers of the name of Moosbrugger, with the help of Italian workmen.   It is the finest thing of its kind in Switzerland, and makes a good pendant to the abbeys just mentioned, more to the Southern German than to the Austrian class ; and in its details is not inferior to the best of those just described.

Out of this last group, built for the most part some few years later than the monasteries on the Danube, the abbey which may be taken as best and most typical of the whole group is Ottobeuren —that is to say, if only one of these can be visited, Ottobeuren, which is still inhabited by monks, should be chosen for preference. These abbeys represent the last great phase of monastic building ; they are the last works of the monks, and where would any country in Europe be without its traces of their handiwork ?   But, apart from this sentiment of homage, Melk or Ottobeuren will come as a revelation of a whole new *world* ; and the pair of them introduce two architects whose names are unknown in this country, Jakob Prandtauer and J. M. Fischer.   The last of these can be placed among the five great architects of Germany ; and I hope that the illustrations given in this book will draw at least a few of my countrymen to Melk and to Ottobeuren, two centres of a prodigious and energetic beauty.

[1] Another work of J. B. Neumann that we mention here at the last opportunity is the Château at Ellingen, ninety miles from Munich on the way to Leipzig.   There is an excellent view of this from the train.   An architect, Franz Keller, built this to his plans about 1718.

III

An Epitome of Painters and Craftsmen

I CANNOT defend the foregoing chapter of this book from a charge of tediousness; it is so loaded with facts and so wearied with the names of towns and architects. But by no other means than a catalogue could this mass of information be dispersed into an accessible form, and now that this is accomplished I can forsake the particular for the general. Baroque and Rococo, those two excessive and interflowing shadows of the classical, merge themselves into an inseparable whole where there is hardly anything save a criterion of scale to distinguish between them. As their definition, then, it will be a simple test to say that the Karlskirche at Vienna is Baroque in style, and that the Johann-Nepomuk church at Munich is frankly and decidedly Rococo. The palaces of Vienna, belonging mostly to the first half of my range of a century, are from their date Baroque; Potsdam, Bruchsal, or Nymphenburg, coming well on into the eighteenth century, are of an indisputable Rococo taste. But the one manner coming after the other should be simple and no matter of difficulty after the slightest experience with the eyes, and there is no necessity to delay here over the obvious any more than there would be in placing an unnecessary emphasis upon the differences between the fullest period of Gothic and the subsequent Perpendicular when dealing with English churches. As regards Germany and Austria the problem of Baroque and Rococo is much more simple than it is in Italy, where the Baroque, alone,

78

went through two or three phases of dry severity and its contrast of theatrical pomposity ; while in Spain and Spanish America there is the Churriguerresque, an entirely novel development leading into the most unimaginable fantasies in Mexico, where this architectural extreme became half Indian and let its detail and ornament evolve from the remains of Aztec symbolism. In Germany and Austria the problem is simplified into a series of developments upon the Roman Baroque of Bernini and Borromini, with its accompanying detail of perspective painting based upon Fratel Pozzo or Bolognese scene-painters like the Bibbiena family. Later on, French workmen and artists brought the influence of Versailles into Germany, and over and above these two foundations there is the natural German consanguinity to the Dutch that has to be reckoned with in an analysis of their achievement. To this extent, then, the problem is simple ; and the subject is difficult because of its magnitude more than for its complexity. There is so much material to be considered, but not a very noticeable divergence from the plain origins mentioned for this plenitude.

If we contrast the German with the French work of the time we find that the age of Louis XIV. had perhaps a stricter and more classical sense of its Cæsarean pretension than is to be found with the Hapsburgs. Louis XIV. justified his affectation by achievement while the House of Austria inherited it, so that we must expect the German nobles to be prouder of their mediæval origins than their French contemporaries. Coats of arms played more of a part in German than in French decoration because the French Court prided itself upon its splendours of modernity and put, therefore, for this reason, a greater insistence upon the present. The Hapsburgs, who were the richest and most powerful of European families over a period of five centuries, we must imagine against an absolute complexity of old fidelities, of paladin-like victories against the Turks, of Spanish relationships ; and their portraits can be placed, for so they would wish them, and so are they to be seen in various palaces and town halls in their dominions, in a series of niches leading directly from Julius Cæsar and through Charlemagne to end with a resigned gentility by Napoleon's side. Even while I write these pages an obituary notice has appeared of an Archduchess of the Hungarian branch of the Hapsburgs, whose husband was a nephew of the last Holy Roman Emperor, so that the ghosts of this strange pretension are hardly cold yet. During their lives they moved in a thicker and more entangled machinery of government than the Bourbons, for a distilled sanctity of inheritance must prove their right to rule over this complex of nations and languages.

Now it must be obvious from every detail mentioned in the previous pages of this book that the art we are discussing is an affair of monasteries and of great or small reigning families. In fact, at its highest development I should say that it comes nearest to perfection when one of those complete fairy-tale worlds of luxury and beauty is reached and a paradise is revealed not unlike the most idealised of hotels in its scope. The eighteenth century is responsible for the creation of several of these in different countries : La Granja in Spain, Queluz in Portugal, Peterhof in Russia, Caserta in Italy, Versailles, of course ; while in Germany and Austria this kind of thing exceeds in its numbers those of all other countries put together, and we can find, to think only of the leading examples, Schönbrunn, Potsdam, Würzburg, Brühl, the Hermitage of Bayreuth, Pommersfelden, and the castles of the Esterházy. Indeed the visual and sensual poetries of life are found in a profusion that would seem not to have the possibility of existence except in music. Those very beautiful and much underrated things, the ballets of Tchaikowsky, have sprung into reality in twenty places, and the person who cannot like *La Belle au Bois Dormant* or *Le Lac des Cygnes* need never be expected to feel the poetry of any of these palaces that I have just mentioned. Anyone who fails here is sincerely to be pitied, for he has missed one of the greatest delights the eyes and the senses can yield him.

An excellent book, only recently published, gives us the whole life of the Elector Clemens Augustus, the builder of Brühl. We see his portraits : he is drinking chocolate in a flowered silk dressing-gown, standing by his chief huntsman, or starting off with his falcons for a day's hunting in the woods. Even his guns have elaborately inlaid or engraved hunting scenes upon their stocks, while a silver stag with heavy antlers is the trigger by which the weapon is fired. We can read his orders to the architects and hear his insistence upon there being room for three hundred horses in his stables ; and the china groups of comedians and crinolined ladies, of shepherds and negro pages, ordered for his dining-table from Meissen or Nymphenburg, are reproduced. He used to go by canal from his castle of Pöppelsdorf to the Falkenlust, a hunting-château not far away, where there was a chapel of Chinese work in which he said Mass. His brother had been elected Holy Roman Emperor as Charles VII., though this honour had soon to be yielded up again to Maria Theresa ; but this family apotheosis, however limited by time, cast the most fervent aura of conviction over the theatrical, but real, properties among which he passed his life.

More strange, and less agreeable, characters there are in plenty ; but luckily the German militarist Princes had little money left over from their expensive game of soldiers, owing to the fabulous cost of uniform and equipment, so that the unpleasant side of German life at that time does not have many claims upon our consideration. The last execution by breaking upon the wheel took place in Germany in 1827, just one hundred years ago, but this survival of mediæval cruelty does not seem to be any worse than the horrors that attended the punishment of the Cato Street conspirators a year before this. England, till the Reform Bill of 1832, was in much the same condition as Germany as regards the lasting of old conventions and old cruelties, so that we must consider the great architects and the great patrons of our period as the true contemporaries of Englishmen of that time, and their works are appropriately warmer and more full of imagination than the cold and Palladian English buildings of the date. It amounts to this, that in considering the German eighteenth century we may put a justifiable stress upon its feudal nature, but it was as "modern" to its own time as England or France, and far from being in that state of perpetual decline into which Spain and Italy had sunk and have not yet emerged. We should be, therefore, very wrong indeed if we regarded this energetic architecture from a patronising point of view as being something provincial as compared with our own contemporary achievement.

In the body of this book five architects—Johann Bernhardt Fischer von Erlach, Lukas von Hildebrandt, Kilian Ignaz Dientzenhofer, J. B. Neumann, and J. M. Fischer—should have emerged into their due prominence, and I suggest that while none of these five is as great a Baroque architect as Bernini or Wren, the least of them has the importance of Juvara or William Kent, this latter an architect who had he been anything but an Englishman would be counted one of the famous names of his country. Beneath them were a host of lesser architects, all of them working along a tradition that hardly allowed anything but excellence to appear; and the designs of all of these were put into execution by an army of talented craftsmen whose taste and technical skill can scarcely have been matched in any country or during any century. But before these latter merits can be discussed a few final remarks must be made about the French or Italian tutelage they underwent.

Rome has already been mentioned as the model upon which German architects tried to improve. The various palaces, churches, and fountains of this city were the familiar and known canons by which the German future was to be judged, and the painted ceilings in palace or church were the apotheoses of painting, if one may judge by the numerous emulations of their splendour that are still to be seen in Central Europe. Bernini exploited his own talent to a degree that makes further progression upon those particular lines almost impossible to imagine ; the Germans were, therefore, wise in enlarging their scope so as to include all that the unsuccessful Borromini might have done had he met with as much patronage, and taken as many opportunities, as his rival. Padre Guarini was considered, in the late Seicento, to be the greatest genius after these two, and Turin, the city in which he worked, had its architecture made still more splendid by a series of buildings of the Sicilian Juvara, who had the greatest name of any architect of his day. Turin was later, and by that much nearer to Vienna, and this city forms an approach to the first Viennese Baroque. Indeed, the Italians began Vienna before the Viennese were ready to embark upon it.

Domenico Martinelli, Ludovico Antonio Burnacini, Fratel Pozzo, these men have already been mentioned in this connection, and they were in this sense the foundation of the Viennese style which had to find some origin from which to be developed into its pointed and particular manner. Martinelli, an architect who came from Lucca, built the Winter and Summer Palaces of Prince Liechtenstein and the Schloss of Prince Kaunitz at Austerlitz; Burnacini has already been indicated as the designer of the Trinity Column in the Graben and has been given due credit for his theatrical genius; but I feel that a few words must be said about Fratel Pozzo, for he had a far-reaching influence and is now little more than a name.

He was born at Trento in 1642 and was therefore a subject of the Emperor of Austria. He was received at an early age into the Jesuit Order and passed his novitiate at Milan, where he seems to have combined being the scullion, or at any rate under-cook, with his other activities. His early works are to be found in Turin in San Carlo, one of the two twin churches in the Piazza San Carlo; in the Badia di San Fiore at Arezzo; and in the Chiesa del Gesu at Montepulciano. His master-piece is the well-known ceiling in the Jesuit church of S. Ignazio at Rome, one of the finest decorative works of all Seicento art and an immeasurably finer performance than the ceiling of the Gesu by Baciccio, with which it is obviously compared, from the fact that these two Jesuit churches in Rome are more or less of the same date and importance. Fratel Pozzo also designed the altar of St Ignatius in the church of that name, and during the many years of his residence in Rome, while he was occupied with these immense works, he painted the corridor outside the cell of St Ignatius in the convent behind the Gesu—an extra-ordinary piece of distorted virtuosity—and during the summers while he was resting in the hills he must have gradually com-pleted the charming ceiling to the Jesuit Church in Frascati. He also painted a highly entertaining series of large water-colours of the life of St Stanislaus Kostka, which are still to be seen in the rooms of this saint behind the church of S. Andrea dell' Quirinale, that masterpiece of Bernini. In 1704 he was invited to Vienna by Prince Liechtenstein, and although, by then, an old man, he did some excellent work in the Prince's Summer Palace, paintings for the high-altar and the six side-altars, as well as for the ceiling and domes of the Old University Church, the high-altar of the Franciscan church, and some pictures for the Dominican church. He died at Vienna in 1709.

Fratel Pozzo was an artist of immense importance during his lifetime and his book on perspective was translated into many languages, including English. He had considerable influence, even in this country, and that able fresco-painter, Sir James Thornhill, drew much profit out of his theories, as can be seen in the painted hall at Greenwich Hospital. The fact that Thornhill's sense of composition was always finer than that of Verrio, or of Laguerre, his two predecessors in this kind of painting, may be put down to the credit of Fratel Pozzo, who had introduced a much more serious and scientific manner of considering the problems likely to baffle the professional panegyrist and the inventor of false architecture. The work of Fratel Pozzo, as we might expect from the years of his life that he passed in Vienna, had a much more lasting influence there than it ever had in England, though there is far more of this Baroque decoration here than is generally admitted, and great houses like Chatsworth, Castle Howard, Blenheim, or Burleigh, cannot be left out of any comprehensive account of this phase of Italian Seicentismo.

The two models out of which a whole host of German artists derived are the ceilings of Fratel Pozzo in the Liechtenstein Summer Palace and his work in the Old University Church. The secular and the religious possibilities of the painted ceiling are set forth in these two places, and a school of painters was soon in existence who practised the apotheosis or the panegyric with a convincing earnestness of intention. But even before these artists were ready the Italians were at work in Vienna: there is a fine ceiling-painting in the Belvedere by Giacomo del Po, the Neapolitan artist; there are fine paintings by Antonio Beduzzi in the Assembly Hall of the Diet of Lower Austria, a superb decoration by Marcantonio Chiarini in the Kinsky Palace, and a charming ceiling, done by Solimena on his visit to Vienna to paint the portrait of Charles VI., decorates the gold-cabinet in the Belvedere.

The chief exponents of this art as regards Vienna were Daniel Gran, 1694-1757, a pupil of Ricci at Venice and of Solimena at Naples; Anton Maulpertsch, 1724-1796; and J. M. Rottmayr, 1652-1730. The first of these, a very considerable artist, painted several ceilings at the Schwarzenberg Palace, worked at the Schloss at Eckartsau on the Danube near Vienna, and frescoed the dome of the Hofbibliothek; Maulpertsch worked at the church of the Piarist Fathers and in various palaces; Rottmayr did frescoes in the Karlskirche, in various Viennese palaces, and in the Residenz at Salzburg. Mention should also be made of Vinzenz Fischer, 1729-1810, who painted in the Temple of Diana in the gardens of the Royal Palace at Laxenburg outside Vienna; of Paul Troger's work in the library at Melk; and finally of the delightful frescoes, from the excellence of the painted architecture and of the costumes and military uniforms, that were done by an Italian, Gregorio Guglielmi, 1714-1773, a pupil of Sebastiano Conca, in the Academy of Science at Vienna (which was formerly the Jesuit convent attached to the Old University Church), and in various rooms at Schönbrunn. Guglielmi was, in fact, an artist as good as Fratel Pozzo or Daniel Gran, but he was later in date, most of his work dating from between 1750 and 1765.

By this time, and before now, other influences beside that of

Fratel Pozzo had begun to assert themselves. The later Neapolitan school of frescoists, coming after the death of Luca Giordano, had much effect, and traces of Francesco di Mura and Sebastiano Conca are to be found on every ceiling and painted decoration. Besides this, there is a strong theatrical flavour due to the presence of so many great stage experts in Vienna, where the Emperor had a hereditary love of music and kept the most highly paid vocalists, instrumental players, dancers and scene-painters that Italy could provide. At least a dozen members of the Bibbiena family must have worked here, and the greatest of them all, Giuseppe Galli Bibbiena, published his huge work, *Archittetture e Prospettive*, at Augsburg in 1740 with a dedication to Charles VI. and with a whole-page portrait of that last male Hapsburg. Many of the scenes that Giuseppe invented and had engraved for his book were executed for this Emperor, and besides these, and the series of catafalques and sacred dramas to be played in churches, there are plates of the Riding-School in Vienna, changed by this inventive genius into the most superb setting for pageantry of an idealised circus nature, like the "carousals" of Louis XIV., where the "haute école" is shown at the highest point to which it ever reached, and something of the same kind as the old Equestrian Drama of Astley's Amphitheatre is seen carried out of circus and melodrama into terms of real art and invention.

This was the Golden Age of theatrical production, and its influences made themselves felt not only in the meretricious but delightful ceiling-painting of that time, but also in the actual architecture ; so that such things as the caryatides of the staircases at the Belvedere, or at Brühl, are the direct outcome of the theatre, and far from being weak or flimsy from this transference of canvas into stone, from something painted into something real, the imaginative possibilities of architecture have been developed into a really suitable setting for that mixture of fabulous elegance and bucolic coarseness from which the German Eighteenth Century was composed. Extreme affectation of manner and personality went with the coloratura singing of the age of Farinelli and with that perfection of dancing which Lambranzi's book upon the subject reveals at the first opening of its pages ; therefore the architecture of that age had to provide a background for these curiosities, and to be suitable for them it must never be of that plain substance against which a crowd of khaki figures, or a mob of factory-workers or shoppers at bargain sales would feel no embarrassment from there being no hint of sarcasm in their surroundings. The high clipped hedges, the staircases that moved with cascades as though a part of their machinery, the lacquered, mirrored, or tapestried walls of rooms, all these things show certain of the human senses carried to their highest pitch of perfection and then strengthened and made more subtle by the illusion of the theatre, which the skill and wealth of that time contrived to change from unreal into real.

To conclude with the ceiling painters of Germany and the Italian influence upon this art mention must be made once again of Rudolf Byss, who designed the Comedian tapestries at Würzburg and worked at Pommersfelden ; and of the two Zicks, whose works are to be seen at Bruchsal and also at Pommersfelden. But now a last wave of energy came from Italy and the great Giambattista Tiepolo was called to Germany, where he did his finest work. The two brothers of the Schönborn family had built the Schloss at Würzburg and it now only required its completion of decoration and furnishing. Prince-Bishop Karl Philipp von Greiffenklau engaged Tiepolo to work for him, and the staircase, the Kaisersaal, and the altarpieces in the Palace-Chapel were all completed by him during the three years—1751-1753—that he remained in the Prince-Bishop's employment. Tiepolo's frescoes at Würzburg are too well known to require reproduction, but it is a pity that no photograph can be given in this book of his pair of easel-pictures showing the journey of Abraham and Lot into Egypt. These two pictures were bought recently from a London dealer and are now in the collection of Senatore L. Albertini in Milan, and it was only on their purchase that the small stone coat of arms painted on the bridge, in one of them, was positively identified as being that of the Prince-Bishop von Greiffenklau. They are little-known specimens of Tiepolo's art and show his genius at one of its most brilliant moments, while they are of interest to our subject from their revelation of what the wealth of German princes could purchase from contemporary Italian talent.

Tiepolo was the last of the great decorators, and his natural style developed out of his admiration of Veronese and of Rubens is seen at Würzburg, and in this pair of pictures which are a small detail of work from his achievement during those three years, in a perfection that is altogether lacking with regard to the other Italian masters of this school. The Germans had the patience and the wealth to carry the Baroque movement to a much higher point than it ever reached in Italy, where poverty had to make plaster stand for stone; but her great decorators, save only for Tiepolo, never worked in Germany. Pietro da Cortona, or Luca Giordano, never went there; though, had they done so, their works would have been surrounded with a much finer setting of architecture and ornament than they ever attained to in Rome, in Florence, in Naples, or at the Escurial. The Pisani Palace at Stra, near Venice, where Tiepolo frescoed the ball-room, is a flimsy and gimcrack affair compared with Würzburg; while, when Tiepolo painted the throne-room at

Madrid he was getting old and his invention was beginning to flag, so that we can say with perfect truth that one of the greatest achievements of Italian decorative painting is to be seen at Würzburg in combination with an architecture that neither Italy nor Spain could afford to construct.

At the date these frescoes were painted Germany had plenty of good architects of her own race and the importation of Italian talent had almost ceased. This was about the period when the palaces at Potsdam were begun, and there is hardly an Italian name connected with their construction. In the Neues Schloss there is a room decorated with framed canvases by Solimena, but, apart from this, every craftsman or artist employed by Frederick the Great was a Frenchman, if he was not a German. It is, therefore, a break in tradition, and following upon this change we find work at Potsdam to be exclusively Rococo, as though the Baroque age was dead and extinct.

This oasis in the sands of Prussia is due entirely to one man, Frederick the Great. His peculiar character, compounded out of thwarted instincts and unlikely talents developed into genius, made him a most fervent Francophil. No man was ever more physically unlike his forbears than Frederick the Great, yet he developed the military tastes that he inherited from his father from being a mere parade-ground martinet into becoming one of the great generals of history. He was politically, as Mr Wyndham Lewis has pointed out, the most complete pattern of what Machiavelli had intended two centuries before, and he made the fullest possible use of that dull, but accurate, machine the Prussian army, over which he found himself in control. His delicate manipulation of this engine showed a refined and perverse brain very unlike any Prussian mind that has existed at any other time, and while using his Prussian inheritance to all this advantage he remained an alien, having thrown himself body and soul into the French traditions of invention and wit. He created a foreign world in which to pass his life and raised this whole town of Potsdam, as the centre of Prussian military life, in the middle of which web of defence he himself lived in the most delicate manner possible, in the most luxurious fitments, but with little personal comfort. This town is only German, then, because it is in Germany; but its character, though its details are so largely the work of Frenchmen, is not French any more than it is German. It possesses something outside and beyond either of these alternatives, and this mystery of its quality is to be ascribed entirely to Frederick.

The three palaces that he built there have already been mentioned earlier in this book, and it was claimed for them that they are the greatest achievement of the Rococo age and are as beautiful as any works of man can be. The perfect technique of the best French craftsmen was employed here upon schemes that offered them a much greater scope than they ever found in their native land. At this time the wilder excesses of the first Rococo had worn off; in order to understand this ebullition of high spirits at the death of Louis XIV. and the dawning of a less severe and classical age it is necessary to have seen the books of designs by Gilles Marie Oppenord, 1672-1742, and Justes Auréle Meissonier, 1675-1750. The first of these two men passed his life in Paris and the second was a native of Turin. The range of their design is astonishing, for a sketch for a silver spoon or a small box is seen side by side with the design of a palace, or the complete interior for some elaborate room designed and made in Paris and then carried to Poland, or to Portugal, and set up there. No line is ever allowed to run straight to its object, and these two masters of the eccentric made out of their art a series of eloquent excuses covering and pardoning everything.

The wilder their designs were the more quickly and expensively were they bought up by the foreign market, and the nobles of Germany, Poland, or Hungary paid out ruinous sums of money in order to bring some corner of their native fastnesses into the fashion of the moment. The millionaires of the Argentine and Brazil in our day are parelleled in that past, and there is no doubt that the French Rococo ran into its wildest moments in order to satisfy this patronage. There were a number of other craftsmen working in Paris who were themselves of foreign origin and who did most of their handiwork for the foreign trade—Servandoni, the famous Caffieri family— these are two more names of artists from whom absolutely any nature of thing could be ordered, from complete churches or palaces down to the smallest objects upon which skill could be lavished.

Unfortunately the very qualities for which such work as this is interesting has meant its destruction, so that far more of it has disappeared than is in existence. In France, itself, there is nearly nothing, and only in Germany is there any survival of these things on a large scale. A town like Nancy, the only thing of its kind in France and one of the wonders of that whole country, would be in competition, were it in Germany, with quite a number of rivals. We shall, then, only be waiting for the truth if we expect to find that Potsdam, or Nymphenburg, are works of the French Eighteenth Century, but in a manner quite transcendentalised out of what is familiar about that style.

Even so, it would be unjust to insist too much upon this

French influence, for while certain concrete instances can be given in which French talent, and nothing else except French talent, was employed, there are more cases where a chief architect or designer of this race had under his directions a number of German craftsmen. Thus Cuvilliés, in his work at Munich, had as assistants such names as Miroffsky and Zimmermann ; the former of these being the Ebeniste who made the furniture that Cuvilliés designed for the Royal Palace in Munich, and the latter the artist who executed most of the lovely stucco designs in the Amalienburg pavilion at Nymphenburg. On the whole this French influence upon Germany can be summed up as follows : the fusion of some French experts working in that extreme manner which they employed for foreign patrons outside France with German craftsmen possessed of the traditional German patience and minuteness of detail created an indigenous style which can be seen in the palaces at Potsdam and at Amalienburg. This style has the qualities of both races and is yet outside what is typical of either ; where for example the Archives in Paris (the former Hôtel de Soubise) may be held for the average of the French style, and Bruchsal, or any good Viennese palace, for the German.

The German gardens of the eighteenth century are of the formal Italian design brought up to date by the inventions of Le Nôtre and the example of Versailles. It is more difficult, though, to account for the beauty of the garden-statues. This branch of art is of entirely Italian invention, beginning, I suppose, with the river-gods and tritons that Vignola designed for Caprarola and Villa Lante, and with John of Bologna's fountain at that latter place. When Versailles was built a whole group of French sculptors were employed to provide the gardens with their complement of statues ; French sculptors made the statues for the great garden at Caserta, and two generations of French sculptors worked at La Granja for the Bourbon Kings of Spain. Most of the statues in the German gardens were apparently the work of itinerant Italians who went from place to place wherever there was work in hand. During a stay at any one place, which was more often than not a matter of several years' work, they had to set up workshops and employ German assistants. In this way a German school of garden-sculptors came quickly into being, though it is hard to distinguish between their work and that of their Italian tutors. The best garden-statues in Germany and Austria are, perhaps, the four groups in the Mirabell Garden at Salzburg, and the host of statues in the garden at Veitshöchheim, near Würzburg. These are all believed to be of direct Italian workmanship ; the name of the sculptor of the Mirabell groups is preserved, but not so much is known about the sculptures at Veitshöchheim. The particular kind of Italian tradition that was at work in this branch of art seems to have been Venetian, and of that school of which Antonio Calegari, 1698-1777, of Brescia, was the foremost exponent, being indeed a kind of translation of Tiepolo into terms of sculpture. There is a bigger population of good garden-statues in Germany than in the whole of the rest of Europe put together, and it is a division of art to which sufficient attention has never yet been paid.

German sculptors of the religious school existed in plenty, and their works have been studied closely in numerous books. The chief men were Raphael Donner, 1693-1741, and the Bavarian Ignaz Günther, 1725-1775. The former of these decorated the staircase in the Mirabell Schloss at Würzburg and made the leaden equestrian statue of St Martin in Hungarian hussar dress that stands in a chapel built to his designs in the Cathedral at Pressburg in Hungary. He produced numberless statues and groups for Austrian churches and convents. Ignaz Günther worked in the group of monasteries that lie between Ulm and Lake Constance, and of which an account was given in an earlier part of this book. He is by far the more interesting sculptor of the two, and works by him are to be seen, as well as in the monasteries mentioned, in the convents at Schäftlarn, Ettal, Fürstenzell, Grafrath, and Weyarn, all of which lie within a few miles of Munich. Günther's bozzetti, or small models in plaster or wood from which he prepared his big groups and figures, are of a peculiar interest, for his inspiration found a quick and eloquent vehicle of expression, and these little sculptures have a rough and feverish speed about them that can be matched nowhere else save in Bernini and in the very finest of the Spanish "mannerist" sculptors.

Other good German sculptors were Balthasar Permoser, who has already been mentioned sufficiently when his Apotheosis of Prince Eugène was described, and Egid Quirin, 1692-1750, the brother of Cosmas Damian, 1686-1739, Asam. He was the best designer of the elaborate church-altars of that day, and examples of his work are to be seen at Diessen, the little convent already mentioned, where there are pictures by Tiepolo and Piazzetta, and at Weltenburg, where there is an amazing altar by him with an equestrian figure of St George conceived and lighted in the most effective manner imaginable. He also made altars at Osterhofen on the Lake of Schliersee, in the monastery at Rohr, near Ingoldstadt, and in the Cathedral at Freising. He and his brother are said to have worked in England, but no traces of their work have so far come to light. His architectural work in conjunction with his brother was mentioned at the end of the previous chapter of this book.

Perhaps a few words more should be said about Andreas

Schlüter in concluding this account of German sculpture. Besides his architectural work, of which the Royal Palace in Berlin is the chief specimen, Schlüter made, in 1701, the well-known equestrian statue of the Great Elector which stands outside the Palace. He was also responsible for a fine bronze bust of Prince Frederick of Homburg in the palace at Homburg, for a series of reliefs in the Berlin Zeughaus, and for some good decorative sculptures in the Royal York Masonic Lodge at Berlin. He was a sculptor whose technique was far in advance of his imagination, and even the Baroque affectations of his day could not conceal an academical smoothness which makes his work vapid and uninteresting.

Should German sculpture be carried down to its smallest details it rises up again into a supreme art of which I am not informed enough to write. The porcelain figures and groups from Dresden are a world in themselves and one into which it is unwise to venture in this casual manner, so that no more is done here than to mention the names of the two directors from whom this creation sprang. They were Johann Joachim Kändler, 1706-1775, and Count Marcolini ; but in finishing this superficial paragraph it must be added that other factories besides that of Dresden produced works of first-rate excellence, notably those of Nymphenburg and Frankenthal. The imagination and the skill seem in all these cases to have been of Italian origin, and this, combined with the patience and the greater wealth of Germany, gave birth to works which the craftsmen of neither country working separately without the other could have produced. In fact, the situation is exactly the same as that described as having been responsible for the palaces at Potsdam and at Nymphenburg.

Having now given some space to the influences of Italy

and France upon Germany there remains the fact that Northern Germany bordered upon Holland, and that the Protestantism of both countries brought them into a cultural and spiritual affinity which made a closer union than that of mere geographical fact. Even now, though, the problem is far from being simple, for two Hollands are concerned, that of the Dutch pictures, Dutch canals, and red-brick houses of The Hague and Amsterdam, and that other Holland of which the importance is not so easily recognised. This is of the Eastern provinces, of Friesland, and of the country-houses of the Dutch nobles round Utrecht, and between that town and the German frontier. Here there is a homogeneous and uniform style, which can be instanced in houses like Rozendaal, and its aristocratic manner is one quite at variance with the customary bourgeois Dutch neatness and smallness. Its effects were far-reaching in Northern Germany in the districts that centred round Mecklenburg, Oldenburg, Hanover, or Brunswick. Belgium, also, had its Baroque architecture, the importance of which is not yet realised. There was at least one great sculptor-architect, Lucas Faid'herbe, 1617-1697, a pupil of Rubens and a native of Malines. In his native town he built the churches of SS. Peter and Paul and Notre Dame D'Hanswyk, and the Jesuit church of St Michael at Louvain. There are, also, the four great Norbertine Abbeys of Ninove, near Ath, Grimberghen, near Brussels, Averbode, near Antwerp, and lastly the Abbaye du Parc, near Louvain, which is a most beautiful building with several remarkable stucco ceilings of peculiar style by an artist whose work is to be seen only here, a fine church, library, Abbot's apartments, and, in fact, all the details that are to be found in the finest German monasteries of the Baroque period.

The Scandinavian countries, though possessing many buildings of this epoch, never exported any of their craftsmen or architects to Germany. Danish work is of either Dutch or French inspiration, the best thing of its kind in that country being perhaps the Amalienborg Square at Copenhagen with its four palaces by Nic. Eigtved that enclose an equestrian statue of Frederik V. (*d.* 1766), by the Frenchman, J. F. J. Saly. The same things are true of Sweden, except that one great native architect was produced, Carl Gustav Tessin, 1694-1771, who was trained in France. It is not necessary to mention more than a very few buildings in this country : the Riddarhus, or House of Peers, in Stockholm, built in 1641-1674 by the Frenchman, Simon de la Vallée ; the Royal Palace, built by Nicodemus and C. G. Tessin, and the Royal Villa of Drottning-holm, a few miles from the capital. Here there are a theatre with many sets of Italian architectural scenery of the utmost interest, and a lovely Chinese pavilion, the Amalienborg, which rivals anything of the kind to be seen in Germany. Nicodemus, the father of C. G. Tessin, was also a talented architect. He studied in Rome under Bernini for four years, and built the Royal castles of Stroemsholm, and Ulriksdal, and the cathedral of Kalmar. His son studied in Paris and was always under French influence ; indeed the fine Bouchers and other French eighteenth-century pictures in the Stockholm gallery are due to his residence in Paris. He also was in negotiation for G. B. Tiepolo to come and paint the hall, known as the White Sea, in the Royal Palace ; but Tiepolo's charges were too high and the work was executed by inferior Italian artists in his stead.

The Russian work of our period is far too big a subject to embark upon in this place, for there is an extraordinary amount of material to be studied. One Italian architect of immense talent, Rastrelli, *d.* 1770, who is somehow seldom included in any survey of the Italian genius, built the Winter Palace in St Petersburgh and the palaces of Tsarsköe Selo and Peterhof outside. At this latter place the fountains and statues are the best contemporary French work that money could procure, rivalling, if not excelling, those of La Granja in Spain. He also designed numerous smaller palaces in St Petersburgh, and the great Smolny convent. There is much interesting work in the old Baltic provinces of Russia that are now independent Republics, but the capital has more of interest with these two enormous palaces, and there are many other Royal villas—at Orenianbaum, for example, and at Gatchina and Strelna. Later on—but this is outside our subject—Giacomo Quarenghi of Bergamo, 1744-1817, and other Italians, introduced the strict classical style which reached its highest achievements in Russia and produced works of wonderful merit up till about the year 1840. The last Italian stage-artists worked in Russia painting scenery for the Imperial theatres, and false-perspectives, or ceilings, for the Imperial villas, and the two last of them, Gonzaga, 1751-1831, and San Quirico, were still employed at this survival of an ancient art till about the year just mentioned. These details of Russia may seem irrelevant to our subject, but they conclude the whole of the Northern Baroque movement, and no book upon the late German Renaissance Architecture would be complete without some closing words upon Rastrelli, an architect of equal talent to that of any of the five great Germans mentioned in this book.

There can be but little that still remains to be added to this catalogue of Northern Baroque Art. In our own country there is little, or nothing ; there is just a trace of its influence among the ruins of Bolsover Castle in Derbyshire, but I do not

think that Vanbrugh has really a place among the great architects
of this school. He was a whole movement to himself, and it
would be most unwise to couple his name with that of Fischer
von Erlach or Lukas von Hildebrandt in any other context than
the mere fact of their having all been in the world at the same
time. We must return, then, out of this wide excursion that
we have undertaken in order to find ourselves back once more
in Germany where we started, and from which it is surprising
that we had the energy to emerge, so vast and unending are the
perspectives down which it is necessary to travel. The material
is much more copious than that offered to us by the England
of the same period; this is because in England the activity
of that time is confined entirely to private houses, the vast
majority of them being country-houses, while, in the German
lands, there are not only these, but also the great palaces of the
nobles in the chief towns, and, over and above this, the huge
ecclesiastical energies of the day, which found their opportunity
in the erection of huge convents and elaborate churches.

The fluent and coloured life of the period found its expression
in that wonderful output of music to which this architecture is
contemporary. But whereas in German music there are only
three or four great names—Handel, Bach, Haydn, Mozart—
and below them nothing which has interested even the most
erudite of connoisseurs, below Fischer von Erlach, Lukas von
Hildebrandt, Kilian Ignaz Dientzenhofer, J. B. Neumann and
J. M. Fischer there is a whole army of architects and of
decorators. Not only are their works of at any rate a secondary
excellence but they have that additional interest that the style
changes according to the locality in which it has been produced,
so that the different kingdoms or principalities of Germany have
subtle differences of manner by which they can be distinguished.

In fact there is as much particularity between them as in Italy, where the profound difference between, for example, the late Renaissance in Venice or in Naples is a great part of the delight that is produced by visiting both these cities.

Germany has for too long been regarded in the light of Luther and of Albert Dürer, and I do not think that anybody who looks at the photographs with which this book is illustrated could deny that they show the German races moving in an environment that is just as suitable to them as the thin Gothic arches and the painfully elaborate wood-carvings of the earlier national style. During the interval between these two creations Germany had grown into an eloquence and a grace that could never have been expected or foreseen out of her earlier Renaissance. The beauty of their music is the key that explains this sudden assumption of qualities that seem so foreign and unlikely to them; in the same way that the recent discoveries of Elizabethan music give a reason and a new force to the works of our great poets. The new eloquence and the enlarged vocabulary of the one had helped the other into expression, and now the mystery is explained even if it is impossible to copy it and make it work.

The utility of such a revelation as regards ourselves is not so easily excused, and I have to fall back upon the explanation of my purpose in a previous book — *Southern Baroque Art*. I prefaced that work with the remark that one of its objects was to extol practically the only art that had not become tarnished with a too extravagant admiration, thus completing the round and leaving our own generation free to follow out their own ideas. That purpose I have extended into this present book with the defence that the subjects of which it treats are perhaps even less known than the corresponding monuments in Italy or

Spain with which the book deals that I wrote four years ago. Indeed, there is so little in our language that even touches upon this period that a plethora of facts and names has made these pages into little better than a catalogue ; it is a list of things more than an interpretation. They are the last affairs of the feudal age in Europe ; the last great building-age of Christianity ; the last flowering of the Renaissance ; and surely these three factors working together have produced an art that is worth this trouble to investigate. This must serve as my excuse, and, at the same time, as my gratitude for the pleasures it has given me.

BIBLIOGRAPHY

No alphabetical or chronological order is attempted. In a short catalogue of this description it has not seemed necessary. The catalogue numbers in the British Museum are given, where possible.

BOOKS PUBLISHED BEFORE 1860

Paulus Decker the Elder: *Fürstlicher Baumeister oder Architectura Civilis*. Augsburg, 1711-1716. 3.Tab.36.
  (An extraordinary work of fantasy, to be compared with the finest plates of Piranesi. The last part of the book, not always found, deals with gardens.)

Andrea Pozzo: *Prospectiva Pictorum et Architectorum*. Rome, 1693-1700. 747.d.25.

Andrea Pozzo: *Rules and Examples of Perspective, proper for Painters and Architects*. Translated by J. James. London, 1707.
  (The English edition of Fratel Pozzo's famous work, with all the illustrations reproduced.)

Salomon Kleiner: *Die Kürfürstlische Mayntzsche Favorite*. 1726.

Salomon Kleiner: *Vera et accurata delineatio omnium templorum et coenobiorum, quae tam in Caesareae urbe ac sede Vienna Austriae*. Augsburg, 1724.
(An immense work. There is a last part, of extreme rarity, dealing with gardens.)

Salomon Kleiner: *La Menagerie de Prince Eugène*. Augsburg, 1734. 460.a.4.

Bibliography

Salomon Kleiner : *Résidences mémorables de l'incomparable héros de notre siècle, Eugène François de Savoie.* Augsburg, 1731. 1734.a.23.
> (Superb views of the Belvedere at Vienna.)

D. M. Poeppelmann : *Vorstellung und Beschreibung des von S. Kgl. Majestät in Pohlen erbauten sog.* Zwinger Gartens Gebäuden. 1729.
> (The plates are enlivened by many splendid figures in Polish dress.)

Johann Andreas Pfeffel : *Triumphus novem seculorum Imperii Romano-Germanici.* 1725. 747.d.21.

Carl Schuetz : *Sammlung von 36 Aussichten der Residenzstadt Wien.* 1779. 12.Tab.48.
> (An album of thirty-six beautifully hand-coloured views of Vienna.)

I. Wachsmuth and C. Ripa : *C. Ripae—Sinnbildern und Gedancken, etc.* Augsburg, 1760 ? 87.k.14.
> (Two plates from this book of emblems are reproduced.)

Gregorio Lambranzi : *Neue und Curieuse Theatrialische Tanz-schül.* Augsburg, 1716.
> (This is the most beautiful theatrical work ever published. Nothing whatever is known of the author's history. It is in two volumes, each containing fifty plates, and, at the beginning, directions for each dance in Italian and German are copperplated.)

Joseph Furtenbach : *Architectura recreationis.* 1640. 1265.f.24. (2).

Joseph Furtenbach : *Architectura Civilis.* 1623. 1265.f.26. (1).

E. G. Happel : *Thesaurus Exoticorum.* 1688. 793.m.9.

Vorstellung und Erklarung Carolo VI. 1741. 813.i.42.

T. Buonaventuri : *Esequie della Maesta Caesarea Leopoldo I.* 1705. 813.f.56.

Bibliography

Fous inexhaustus immortalis gloriae Carolus—Bohemiae Dux. 1723. 1864.a.4.

    (This curious book, published by the Jesuits of Bohemia, contains many beautifully engraved fountains emblematic of the Hapsburg virtues and the benefits conferred by their rule.)

Memoria gloriosa regiae stirpis Habspurgicae. 1709. 9314.aa.2.

    (This is a magnificent work, consisting of huge engraved triumphal arches surmounted with statues of the Hapsburgs. Nothing more far-fetched than this could be imagined.)

M. J. F. W. *Das hochbeerte Augsburg : Josephi primo.* 1690. 9930.dd.2. (2).

PIERRE DE BRETAGNE : *Rejouissances et fêtes magnifiques en Bavière.* 1723. 9930.h.38.
    (Fine plates of fireworks.)

Vollständiges Diarium Carol des VII. 1742. 9930.i.13.

Imago Caesaris Leopoldi Magni. 1690? 10795.f.20. (5).

HANS VON FRANCOLIN : *Thurnier-Bach.* 1561. 608.K.15. (2).

    (Many fine plates of tournaments, some of them held in the court of the Hofburg at Vienna.)

Wunderwürdiges Leben und Gross-Thaten Caroli Sechsten. 1721. 1204.c.25.

Fröhliches Zujauchzen an den allerdauchlaüchtigsten—Herren-Carlen VI. 1712. 9315.f.9. (2).

Pompe funèbre de Charles VI. 1741. 9930.g.3. (1).

Beschreibung, wie es bey der Kaysers Caroli. 1723. 813.h.47. (1).

Plenitudo dierum—Josephus I. 1711. 10795.f.20. (6).

J. A. PFEFFEL : *Physique sacrée.* 1732. 459.d.17.

JOHANN BERNHARDT FISCHER VON ERLACH : *Entwurff einer historischen Architektur.* Vienna, 1721. 648.a.3.

Bibliography

JOHANN BERNHARDT FISCHER VON ERLACH : *A Plan of Civil and Historical Architecture.* Translated by T. Lediard. Second edition. London, 1737. 60.g.8.

(The English edition with all the plates reproduced.)

GIUSEPPE GALLI BIBBIENA : *Archittetture e Prospettive.* Augsburg. 1740. 559.h.16.

(This is the most sumptuous and magnificent work on perspective, on church ceremonies, and on the theatre.)

MODERN AUTHORITIES

DR EDMUND RENARD : *Clemens August, Kürfurst von Koln.* Vilhagen Verlag. Leipzig, 1927.

(An excellent book, giving the life and the whole surroundings of the builder of Brühl. The illustrations are beyond praise.)

HERMANN POPP : *Die Architektur der Barock- und Rokoko-zeit in Deutschland und der Schweiz.* Stuttgart, 1913.

MAX VON BOEHN : *Deutschland im 18 Jahrhundert.* Berlin, 1921.

HERMANN SCHMITZ : *Kunst und Kultur des 18 Jahrhunderts in Deutschland.* Munich, 1922.

HANS TIETZE : *Domenico Martinelli.* Vienna, 1923.

DAGOBERT FREY : *Johann Bernhardt Fischer von Erlach.* Vienna, 1923.

BRUNO GRIMSCHITZ : *Johann Lukas von Hildebrandt.* Vienna, 1923.

DR HANS SEDLMAYER : *Fischer von Erlach.* Vienna, 1925.

BERNARDUS SCHURR : *Das alte und neue Munster in Zwiefalten.* 1910.

H. S. LEVETUS : *Imperial Vienna.* London. John Lane. 1905.

Bibliography

W. Kick ; Q. B. Pfeifer : *Barock und Rokoko in Schwaben und der Scheiz.* 1907. 61.k.(S.K.M.).

Adolf Feulner : *Bayerisches Rokoko.* Kurt Wolff Verlag. Munich. 1923.
> (This is a superb publication, especially interesting for its photographs of churches by J. M. Fischer.)

Dr Hugo Schmerber : *Beiträge zur Geschichte der Dientzenhofer.* Prague, 1900.

Monumenta Scenica : A series of twelve volumes to be published from Vienna showing the finest treasures of theatrical art found in the Hofburg Library at Vienna, where they had for long lain unknown and uncared for. Seven volumes have already appeared, including the designs for costumes by Ludovico Antonio Burnacini, silverpoints of dresses by Antonio Bertoli, volumes of architectural and garden scenery by the Bibbiena and Burnacini, and the *carrousels* of Louis XIV. illuminated in gold and colours after Israel Sylvestre. The series is edited by Josef Gregor.

Hans Sedlmayer : *Das Würzburger Residenz.*
> (This is the great authority on Würzburg and on J. B. Neumann.)

Hugo Hautsch : *Jakob Prandauer.* Krystall-Verlag. Vienna, 1926.
> (An excellent book on the architect of Melk.)

Georg Dehio : *Geschichte der Deutschen Kunst.* Walter de Gruyter & Co. Berlin, 1926.
> (Magnificently illustrated.)

Werner Weisbach : *Baroque Kunst.* A volume in the Propylaean series from Munich.
> (This is the finest art series, as regards illustration, that has ever been published.)

Bibliography

The series of Süddeutsche and Oesterreichische Kunstbücher published by Ed. Hölzel of Vienna contain volumes with good illustrations on the Wiener Hofburg, Stift Göttweig, Schönbrunn, Ottobeuren, Zwiefalten, der Barocken Deckenmalerei in Wien, Stift Klosterneuburg, Johann Michael Fischer, etc. etc.

J. HOLLNSTEINER : *Stift St Florian.*

HEINRICH SCHACHNER : *Das Benediktinerstift Kremsmünster.*

P. AUGUSTIN PLAPPERT : *Das Benediktinerstift Seitenstetten.*

ACKNOWLEDGMENTS

My thanks are due for permission to reproduce the under-mentioned plates as follows :—

PLATES XXV., XXVI., XXVII.

HERMANN SCHMITZ : *Kunst und Kultur des 18 Jahrhunderts in Deutschland.*

PLATE XXVIII.

The Illustrated Catalogue of the Baroque Museum in the Belvedere, Vienna.

PLATES XXXII., XXXIII., XXXIV., XXXV., XXXVI., XXXVII., XXXVIII., XXXIX., XLIV., XLV.

HERMANN POPP : *Die Architektur der Barock- und Rokoko-zeit in Deutschland und der Schweiz.* Stuttgart, 1913.

PLATES XLI., XLII.

MAX VON BOEHN : *Deutschland im 18 Jahrhundert.* Berlin. 1921.

PLATES XLIII., XLVII.

ADOLF FEULNER : *Bayerisches Rokoko.* Munich. 1923.

PLATES XXIX., XXX., XL., XLVIII.

GEORG DEHIO : *Geschichte der Deutschen Kunst*, 1926, and for Plate XXXI., to the Abbot of Kremsmünster.

A

P. Decker Archit. invent. et del.

Bfinowich Arnio Aureloo Sculpsit

Paulus Decker the Elder.

I. GATEWAY TO A PALACE.

Paulus Decker the Elder.

2. A PALACE.

3. A PALACE GARDEN.

Paulus Decker the Elder.

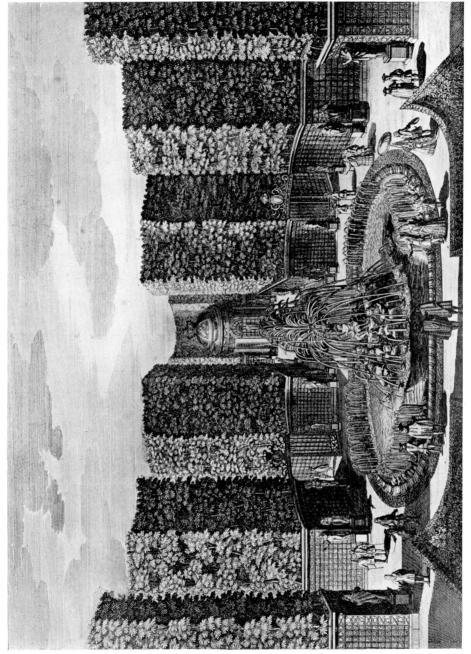

4. A FOUNTAIN.

Paulus Decker the Elder.

Paulus Decker the Elder.

5. A GARDEN.

Wachsmuth and Ripa.

6. Book Illustration.

Pars IVta
Historiæ
et
Allegoriæ
Projectæ et designatæ
a
Gottfr. Eichler, jun.
Excusæ
ab Authore
Joh. Georgio
Hertel,
Aug Vind.

J. Wachsmuth Sculps.

Wachsmuth and Ripa.

7. BOOK ILLUSTRATION.

Salomon Kleiner.

8. CONVENT OF THE THEATINES, VIENNA.

9. PALACE OF COUNT THAUN, PRINCE OF THIANO, VIENNA.

B

10. THE OLD RATHAUS, VIENNA.

Salomon Kleiner.

11. PALACE OF PRINCE EUGENE, VIENNA.

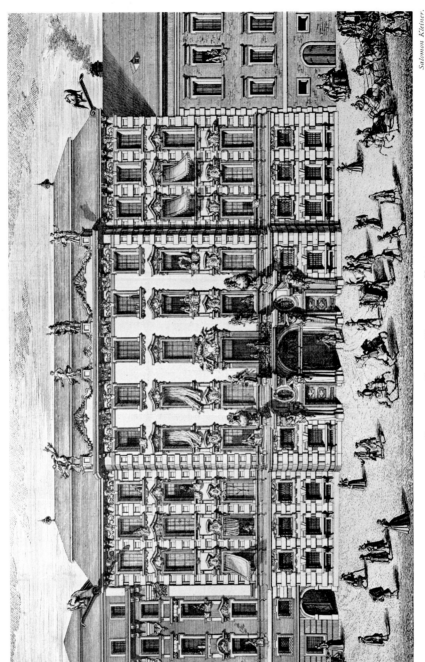

12. PALACE OF PRINCE NEUPAUER, VIENNA.

Salomon Kleiner.

13. The Hofburg, Vienna.

Veue de Sallon ouvert du coté
du grand Escalier

Öffner Saal, gegen der Haupt=Treppen
anzusehen

Salomon Kleiner Jnv: Exc: Maÿ: delin

Cum P: S: Sac: Cæs: Maÿ: Haered: Ier: Wolffÿ excud: A V

Lac contulit Thelot Sculpsit

Salomon Kleiner.

14. ENTRANCE TO THE BELVEDERE, VIENNA.

Vue du grand Escalier. Prospect der Haupt = Treppen.

Salomon Kleiner Fecit delin.

Cum Pr. Sac. Cæs. Maj. Hered. der Wolffg. exc. A.V.

Jacob Gottlieb Thelot Sculpsit.

Salomon Kleiner.

15. STAIRCASE OF THE BELVEDERE, VIENNA.

C. Schütz.

16. THE HOFBIBLIOTHEK, VIENNA.

C. Schütz.

17.   THE BELVEDERE, VIENNA.

C

18. SCHÖNBRUNN.

C Schütz.

19. LIECHTENSTEIN SUMMER PALACE, VIENNA.

Bernardo Bellotto.

20. LIECHTENSTEIN SUMMER PALACE, VIENNA.

Sig: Greg: Lambranzi
Maestro di Balli.

NEUE und CURIEUSE
THEATRIALISCHE
TANTZ, SCHUL
Zweiter theil.
Nürnberg verlegt von
Joh Jacob Wolrab.

21. Portrait of Gregorio Lambranzi in Costume.

Bey Eröffnung der Bühne Presentiret sich diese Figur,
welche im herauß gehen gewieße Contretemps mit
ziehung der knie und füße macht, die übrige
nöthige pas aber sind N.° 34 zu finden.

Gregorio Lambranzi.

22. A DANCE FOR MEZZETIN.

23. ITALIAN COMEDIAN TAPESTRY, WÜRZBURG.

By *Rudolf Buss*.

24. ITALIAN COMEDIAN TAPESTRY, WÜRZBURG.

25. LEOPOLD I. IVORY STATUETTE.

Jacob van Schuppen.

26. CHARLES VI.

Solimena.

27. CHARLES VI.

28. APOTHEOSIS OF PRINCE EUGENE.

Burnacini and Fischer von Erlach.

29. THE TRINITY COLUMN IN THE GRABEN, VIENNA.

30. MELK FROM THE DANUBE.

31. THE FISH-PONDS AT KREMSMÜNSTER.

32. Potsdam, the Town Palace.

33. POTSDAM, MUSIC ROOM IN THE NEW PALACE.

E

34. POTSDAM. SANSSOUCI.

35. HEINRICHAU, SILESIA. CISTERCIAN MONASTERY.

36. DETAIL OF A CEILING IN THE SCHLOSS AT WÜRZBURG.

37. POMMERSFELDEN, STAIRCASE.

38. Kloster Ebrach, Bamberg, Staircase.

39. BRUHL, COLOGNE. FOOT OF STAIRCASE.

40. BRÜHL, COLOGNE. STAIRCASE.

41. FULDA, THE ORANGERY.

42. Kloster Ebrach. Wrought-iron Gate.

43. ZWIEFALTEN. CHOIR-STALLS.

44. Ottobeuren. Church Interior.

45. OTTOBEUREN, CHURCH INTERIOR.

46. OTTOBEUREN, KAISERSAAL.

47.   INGOLSTADT.   INTERIOR OF THE SODALITY CHAPEL.

C. D. and E. Q. Asam.

48. Ingolstadt. Ceiling of the Sodality Chapel.

C. D. Asam.